C000220643

35

Tenerife Walks

David Brawn
Ros Brawn

DISCOVERY WALKING GUIDES LTD

35 Tenerife Walks

First published - March 2003
Copyright © 2003

Published by
Discovery Walking Guides Ltd
10 Tennyson Close, Northampton NN5 7HJ,
England

Maps
Maps are adapted from **Tenerife Walkers' Maps**
published by **Discovery Walking Guides Ltd**

Photographs
All photographs in this book were taken by the
authors, David Brawn and Ros Brawn.

Front Cover Photographs

Walk C2, Arenas Negras - Black Sand Surprise
(top)
Walk W3, True Grit

Rear Cover Photographs
(from top)
View from the Degollada de Guajara taken on Walk
C7, Mighty Guajara
Santiago del Teide as seen from the *ermita*, Walk
W1, Wild West Tour
The Orotava Valley seen from Walk N6, King of the
North
Wow! Spectacular, Walk S10

ISBN 1-899554-38-6

Text, maps and photographs © David & Ros
Brawn 2003

35 Tenerife Walks

Contents

CENTRAL HIGH ALTITUDE REGION

CENTRAL HIGH ALTITUDE WALKS

TENERIFE WEST

WESTERN WALKS

THE AUTHORS

David & Ros Brawn

David and Ros have lived and worked in England, Papua New Guinea and the Seychelles before settling for a number of years in Tenerife. David's first published books were accountancy texts.

David and Ros have been walking and writing for Discovery Walking Guides since it began, researching guides for most of the Canary Islands, the Balearic Islands, Malta, Gozo, Madeira, and the Alpujarras. More recently they have surveyed and mapped a number of these regions using satellite navigation equipment combined with cartographic software.

Considering themselves as semi-permanent travellers, they divide their non-research time between Spain and Northampton, England.

David is a member of the British Cartographic Society.

FOREWORD

It all started as a little walk designed to promote the BookSwop. Called 'Geranium Walk', it started in Los Cristianos and wound its way along the coastal promenade all the way to what was then the far end of Playa de las Américas at Puerto Colón Marina and the BookSwop. That was in 1988, and so popular did this route become that the authorities have officially named the promenade 'Geranium Walk'.

Discovery Walking Guides began as a series of occasional walks in BookSwop newsletters. From these humble beginnings it was soon clear that people wanted more, and the first two 'Warm Island Walking Guides', Tenerife North and Tenerife South, were published, including painstakingly hand-drawn maps.

Being resident in Tenerife, it was logical for us to expand the WIWG titles to include other Canary Islands. 'OS' equivalent map sections were licenced from the Spanish authorities, at a cost, releasing time for research though the maps were often out of date and needed correction by DWG. New titles were added steadily, including publications for La Gomera, Gran Canaria, Lanzarote, El Hierro and La Palma. Inevitably, destinations further afield joined the stable; Mallorca, Ibiza and Menorca in the Balearic Islands, Malta and Gozo, Madeira, The Alpujarras; and the first outside walking authors were taken on to research and write guides for the Algarve. Since then, authors for the new Alpujarras and Lanzarote titles have joined DWG. The format of the walking guides has developed from simple folded maps and walking descriptions, to the current book format that you are now reading, and the '34 Walks' Series.

Cartography
As the company expanded, it became more obvious that the quality of existing maps left a lot to be desired. The answer was clear - DWG would become cartographers, taking on the research and mapping of the walking areas. This steep learning curve was made easier by the miracle of surveying systems based on satellite navigation technology and the new cartographic software. Combine these with the vast increases in portable computer power and you have the mobile ground survey systems that we use today.

The map data collected was not only ideal for enhancing walking guides; the new maps were in demand as publications in their own right, and so 'Tour & Trail Maps' were launched. Since then, 'Drive! Maps' have joined the publication lists, and more recently maps printed on virtually indestructible materials, including titles published by The Indestructible Map Company.

Research
All the walking routes contained in this book have been walked by the authors and are recorded on our mobile ground survey system. Edited versions of the ground survey, taking out the getting lost/false trails/routes which didn't work out, are available as Personal Navigator Files for GPS users with compatible GPS software. We really can prove exactly where our research has taken us, unlike some walking publications we come across. All DWG authors are now required to compile their routes using our mobile ground survey system, guaranteeing that all routes have been walked by the author.

Feedback
When new editions are prepared, it is with the assistance of input by many of the users of DWG's maps and guides. No matter how carefully prepared a publication may be, as soon as it is published some changes inevitably take place - a dirt track is sealed with tarmac, a bar changes its name, a walk is re-routed because of landslip or new fences. Feedback from users can be added to newsletters and DWG websites, until new editions are published which incorporate the updates.

Write to:-

DWG Ltd.
10 Tennyson Close
Northampton NN5 7HJ
England

David & Ros Brawn

LOCATION MAPS

General area covered by the walks in the central - High Altitude area of Tenerife - see detailed location map on page 46.

General area covered by the walks in the west of Tenerife - see detailed location map on page 74.

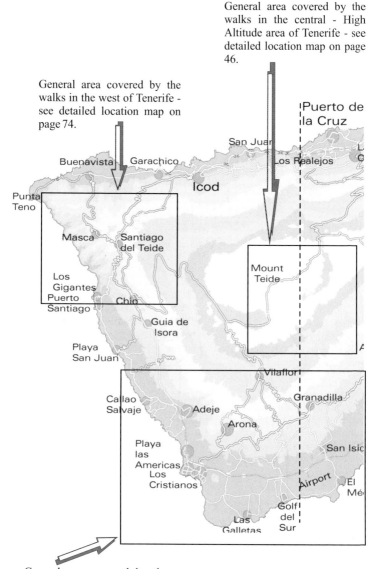

Puerto de la Cruz

San Juan

Los Realejos

Buenavista   Garachico

Icod

Punta Teno

Masca   Santiago del Teide

Los Gigantes
Puerto Santiago   Chio

Mount Teide

Guia de Isora

Playa San Juan

Vilaflor

Callao Salvaje   Adeje   Granadilla

Arona

Playa las Americas
Los Cristianos   San Isic

Airport   El Mé

Golf del Sur

Las Galletas

General area covered by the walks in the south of Tenerife - see detailed location map on page 103.

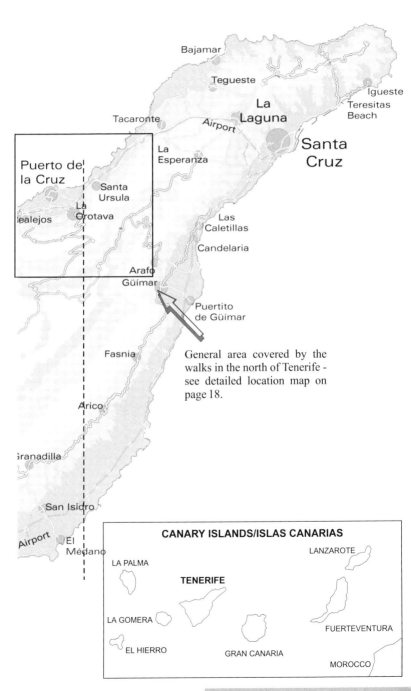

Bajamar

Tegueste

Igueste

Teresitas
Beach

La
Laguna

Tacaronte

Airport

Santa
Cruz

Puerto de
la Cruz

La
Esperanza

Santa
Ursula

La
Orotava

ealejos

Las
Caletillas

Candelaria

Arafo
Güimar

Puertito
de Güímar

Fasnia

General area covered by the
walks in the north of Tenerife -
see detailed location map on
page 18.

Arico

Granadilla

San Isidro

Airport

El
Médano

CANARY ISLANDS/ISLAS CANARIAS

LANZAROTE

LA PALMA

TENERIFE

LA GOMERA

FUERTEVENTURA

EL HIERRO

GRAN CANARIA

MOROCCO

The map sections used in **35 Tenerife Walks** are greyscale versions adapted from **Tenerife Walkers' Maps** published by Discovery Walking Guides Ltd. In the interests of clarity, not all waypoints referred to in the walk descriptions are shown on the map sections.

Tenerife Walkers' Maps contain 1:25,000 full colour topographical maps covering all the regions explored by **35 Tenerife Walks**, and are available in conventional paper and super-durable (waterproof and tear-proof) editions. For more information on DWG publications write to Discovery Walking Guides Ltd, 10 Tennyson Close, Northampton NN5 7HJ, England or visit:
www.walking.demon.co.uk and **www.dwgwalking.co.uk**

Map Legend

Roads, tracks and trails

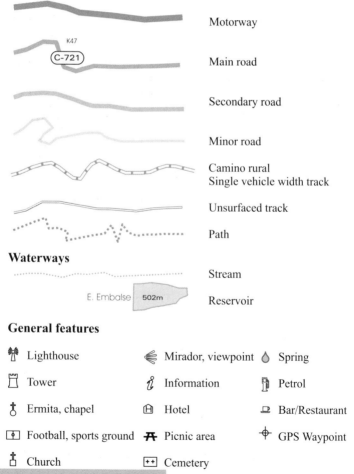

Motorway

Main road

Secondary road

Minor road

Camino rural
Single vehicle width track

Unsurfaced track

Path

Waterways

Stream

Reservoir

General features

🕯 Lighthouse   🎐 Mirador, viewpoint   💧 Spring

🏰 Tower   ℹ️ Information   🅿 Petrol

⚲ Ermita, chapel   🏨 Hotel   🍴 Bar/Restaurant

⚽ Football, sports ground   🪑 Picnic area   ✦ GPS Waypoint

⛪ Church   ⛼ Cemetery

35 Tenerife Walks routes include GPS Waypoints. These refer to specific points along each walking route. A full GPS Waypoint list is provided for each walking route (except where GPS coverage is poor), although not all waypoints are shown on the maps. To use these GPS Waypoints, remember to set your **GPS datum** to **Pico las Nieves**; this datum may be referred to as Canary Islands or Islas Canarias on some GPS receivers. Using the wrong datum can result in significant errors in location.

GPS Waypoints are given in **Latitude/Longitude** coordinates; e.g. start of Barranco del Infierno behind Otello's Bar is Wp.1 28 07.491 N (Latitude) and 16 43.316 W (Longitude). When inputting the Waypoints to your GPS, do remember to have your GPS set to Pico las Nieves datum.

GPS Waypoints are approximate positions, and while we quote positions to 0.001 minutes of arc (approximately 1 metre accuracy) in practice 0.010 minutes of arc (10 metres) is an acceptable standard of accuracy. Note that on the map sections for each walk the GPS Waypoint symbol is placed alongside the walking route for clarity, not on the exact location to which it refers.

Waypoints alone are no substitute for an accurately written walk description, but will ensure that you know when you reach particular points in the walk description and that you are heading in approximately the right direction. Discovery Walking Guides are developing 'Personal Navigator Files' for all their new walking guide books, providing full GPS track and waypoint information for each walking route. These 'Personal Navigator Files' can be downloaded to your GPS receiver, via GPS software, so that you walk in the same footsteps as the author of the guide book. More information on 'Personal Navigator Files' is available on DWG's websites:

www.walking.demon.co.uk and **www.dwgwalking.co.uk**

- GPS Waypoints are provided for each route description in **35 Tenerife Walks** *(with the exception of route W8, 'Survival Of The Fittest', where accuracy is poor due to the extreme nature of the landscape). The waypoint numbers in these lists correspond to the numbers quoted in each walk description, and are for the direction in which the authors describe the route.

- When inputting GPS Waypoints to your GPS receiver, do make sure that you have **set the datum to Pico las Nieves**; possibly known as Canary Islands or Islas Canarias datum on some receivers. Also see 'Navigation and GPS' (above) which provides more information.

- Note that not all GPS Waypoints are shown on the maps, and those that are shown are placed alongside the route rather than at the exact location.

- While we quote GPS Waypoints to 0.001 (1 metre) in practice 0.010 (10 metres) is an acceptable standard of accuracy. GPS Waypoints are extremely difficult to reproduce exactly while on a walking route, unless you spend some time at each waypoint location finding the exact position at which we were holding the GPS unit; hence the 10 metre accuracy for reproducing waypoints in the field or on the mountain.

- Some walking routes have problems with the 'mountain shadowing' effect which reduces GPS reception below four satellites:
- N4, Chimoche Loop on the climb up to Lomo Los Brezos.
- N5, Los Organos around the 'hand rail' and in some ravines.
- C1, Toffee Mountain approaching pista Siete Cañadas.
- W5 Laurel & Hardy deep in the Laurel forest.
- W6 Saddle Up on pista below Pico de Gala.
- W8, Survival Of The Fittest *see walk introduction.
- S2, Barranco del Infierno when deep into the canyon
  S8, Adeje Skywalker on the vertiginous section either side of the aqueduct crossing the Barranco del Agua.

- At all other times on **35 Tenerife Walks** routes, you should have good GPS reception with four or more satellites in view, even in the pine forest.

SYMBOLS RATING GUIDE

- our rating for effort/exertion:
1 very easy   **2** easy
3 average   **4** energetic
5 strenuous   **6** very strenuous

- approximate time to complete the walk (compare your times against ours early in a walk) Does not include picnic stops, etc.

- approximate walking distance in kms

- approximate ascents/descents in metres

- from **0** (none available), up to **5** (exceptional food/drink/position)

Tenerife is a big island - 2034 square kilometres big. It offers the walker a wide variety of landscapes to choose from; everything from coastal strolls, high altitude summits, pine forests and laurel forests, challenging and strenuous routes to easy country walks.

Your choice or routes will most probably be influenced by where you are based. Major roads are generally of a good standard, and public bus services are efficient, clean and reliable. Taxis are reasonable value. Even so, to travel for two or three hours to reach a walk (and back again) can be tedious, so it is best to choose your accommodation to suit your walking needs. For similar reasons, this book omits routes in the least accessible areas of the island, such as the **Anaga Mountains** in the extreme north-east - beautiful but remote with very limited bus services and almost no accommodation.

Walking in the North
The original tourist area of Tenerife offers accommodation of all types around **Puerto de la Cruz** giving easy access to the **Orotava Valley** which climbs up from the north coast until it meets the northern reaches of the **Parque Nacional de Teide**. In addition to the coastal walks in this area, most of which are clearly sign-posted and easy to follow (ask in the local Tourist Offices), the area around **La Caldera**, **Aquamansa**, **La Florida** and **Santa Ursula** offers plenty of walks through pine forests, along forest tracks and walking trails, with fine views in clear weather.

Walking in Central Tenerife
If you want to stay in the centre, there is only one choice; the **Parador Nacional**. Otherwise you can reach **Las Cañadas** by public bus from **Puerto de la Cruz** on the north coast, or from **Playa de las Américas** in the south. Drivers will usually find parking near the walking routes. Our walks include some of the most exciting mountain and *cañadas* routes within the National Park and also two contrasting 'Lunar Landscape' routes .

Walking in the West
Our exciting mountain routes and rugged country walks in this unspoiled side of the island can be reached by bus from the northern and southern resorts, and from the west coast resort areas of **Los Gigantes**, **Playa Santiago** and **Playa de la Arena**. Drivers may have problems finding parking near **Masca** for our 'Survival Of The Fittest' route, and at the start of 'Picnic At Hanging Rock', so start out early.

Walking in the South
There is plenty of accommodation in the sunny southern resorts from **Los Cristianos**, **Playa de las Américas** and to **Playa Fañabe**, and plenty of variety for walkers. Our routes offer coastal discoveries, forest walks, mountains and *barrancos*, villages and untouched wild countryside. Experience our 'Wow! Spectacular', Adeje Skywalker', Taucho Tour' routes (and the rest), and we guarantee that Tenerife South will never seem the same again.

SAFETY

Safety is all about how you walk, and what you take with you. Start with suitable equipment, especially footwear (comfortable, good grip, tough) and sun protection (high factor cream, hat). Dangerous situations can arise through :-

- **Lack of concentration**; always 'Look where you are stepping, and STOP to look at the view'.
- **Tiredness**; walk within your physical limit, and when on strenuous routes, stop and rest whenever you feel the need to recover. This is *not* a race.
- **Sunburn/sunstroke**; wear suitable clothing, hat and sunglasses and high factor sun cream. You can walk in the sun, but always try to rest in the shade.
- **Dehydration**; drink lots of water before, during and after walking.
- **Keep to the route**; even experienced walkers can get lost in unfamiliar terrain.
- **Keep others informed**; let someone responsible know where you are going.
- **If the route ahead is impassable, or if bad weather sets in**; turn back and retrace your steps to the start point.

WHAT TO TAKE

We suggest you take a daypack on any walk. Here's our basic packing list:-

guide book/map

GPS and/or **compass**

2 x ½ litre bottles water per person

snack

lightweight waterproof **jacket**

hat (functional, not Ascot)

sunglasses

plasters

antiseptic cream or wipes

tweezers (for cactus spines)

whistle

camera

secateurs (for overgrown routes)

money (folding and change)

taxi phone numbers

mobile phone

bus timetable

Tenerife's pleasant climate is one of the main reasons that its tourism industry is so successful. It is unusual for the temperature to drop below 16°C in the winter - if you can call it that - or much above 32°C in midsummer (July to mid-September). As a general rule of thumb, the north of the island is cooler and damper than the south and west, and the central region is generally dry but has a greater range of temperature. From the walker's point of view, the summer months are not ideal for tackling anything but short, undemanding walks with plenty of shade along the route.

From September onwards, the temperatures begin to ease and become ideal for walking, although the sun is still strong and must be treated with respect. Always remember to protect yourself from the sun, and to take (and drink) plenty of water, whenever you walk. The climate remains good for walking from around September up until June (approximately), with few exceptions.

When the rains do come to Tenerife, they can be dramatic, particularly in the north. For most of the year you can almost guarantee that rain will not fall, but from November to February there can be the occasional powerful electrical storm, accompanied by torrential downpours that always catch the authorities unawares (the Canarian version of 'leaves on the line'). If you are planning a winter walk in Tenerife's south, west or central regions, and the skies are leaden and the winds blustery, especially from the south-west or north-west, it may well be best to postpone your plans. But even in winter, you would have to be unlucky to experience more than two or three consecutive wild, wet days. However, in the wetter north, several periods of consecutive wet days in winter is usual. Do bear in mind that walking routes may be disrupted after severe weather. Even when you have started out on a perfect day, be aware that the weather on any island, and particularly if you are walking at altitude, is liable to rapid change. Be prepared to abandon your walk and retrace your steps if bad weather threatens.

A few times each year, the island is affected by an unpleasant *sirocco* wind (locally also called *calima*) from Africa; it is hot and laden with Saharan sand and dust which slowly falls and gets everywhere. The temperature rises and stays high, and visibility is reduced. It would be foolish to choose to inhale any more of this air than is necessary, so it is best to avoid walking at these times.

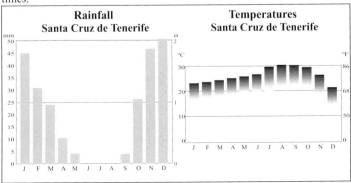

TENERIFE'S GREEN NORTH

Looking north across the Orotava Valley.

Tenerife's long affair with tourism began in **Puerto de la Cruz**, the coastal town which sits on the island's north coast under the shadow of **Montaña Teide**. Behind **Puerto** lies the huge sweep of the **Orotava Valley**, its basin strewn with countless white houses. Roads twist steeply up from the coastal routes, passing through small towns and villages and into the northern regions of the **Parque Nacional del Teide**.

There are some easy and pleasant coastal walks near the resort areas on the north coast, most of which are well marked by the authorities - ask in the tourist offices for information, although you will need little help to follow these routes.

Our northern routes concentrate on country walks in the upper **Orotava Valley**, and walking trails and *pistas forestales* in the pine and laurel forests of the National Park. These walks take you away from the heavily populated lower levels of the **Orotava Valley** and into the northern fringes of the **Parque Nacional del Teide**, with a combination of forest and countryside walks including a taste of some of the higher level villages. The start points of the walks are easily accessed by car drivers, or use the frequent and reliable TITSA bus services to **Aguamansa** and **La Caldera** from **Puerto de la Cruz**.

Northern Tenerife is the greenest part of the island, and the soil in many northern areas is rich and productive. Agriculture is an important industry, and many types of fruits, vegetables and flowers are grown for domestic use and for export. Banana plantations still thrive on the outskirts of **Puerto de la Cruz**, while tomato and potato fields are common as you climb away from the coast, along with grape terraces, often still cultivated in traditional style.

La Caldera

The entire **Orotava Valley** has an air of fertility, thanks not only to its soil, but also thanks to its moist climate, but this can frustrate walkers who may be unfortunate enough to experience two consecutive weeks or more of wet weather in winter and early spring. Walkers should also bear in mind that routes can be made impassable or unsafe at such times.

The forests encountered on our routes are a mixture of Canarian pines and remnants of the ancient laurel forest (including *Laurus azorica*, similar to the bay tree and *Persea indica*), punctuated by groves of eucalyptus. Tree heathers (*Erica arborea*) are commonly seen, as are pink cistus, and the white-flowered broom *Chamaecytisus proliferus*, and a yellow broom, *Teline canariensis*. The dampest parts of the forest where the sun rarely shines are hung with beards of lichen, and the rocks are covered in emerald green moss cushions.

Cistus symphytifolius

The forests are home to several species of birds, easily heard but not so easily spotted. However, patient bird watchers should be rewarded for their vigilance around the **La Caldera** car parking area and the café, where many varieties compete for the crumbs left by visitors. Look out for the Blue Chaffinch (*Fringilla teydea*) Canary (*Serinus canaria*) and Chiffchaff (*Phylloscopus collybita*) in such spots. Numerous insect species thrive in the upper **Orotava Valley** and the National Park, including several showy butterflies, and you will hear (if not see) lizards scuttling in the fallen leaves.

Ⓐ Walk 1
   Flora Loop

Ⓑ Walk 2
   Downhill To
   La Florida

Ⓒ Walk 3
   Choza
   Classic

Ⓓ Walk 4
   Chimoche
   Loop

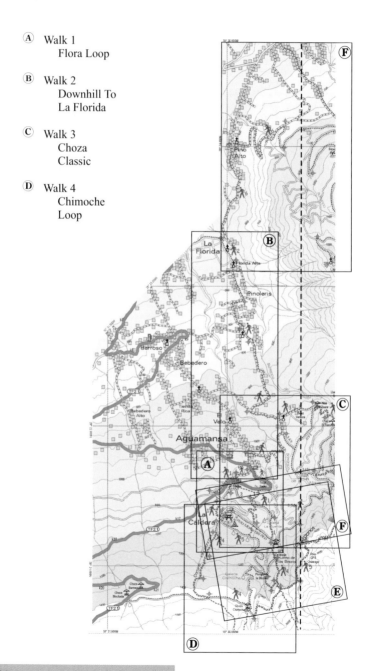

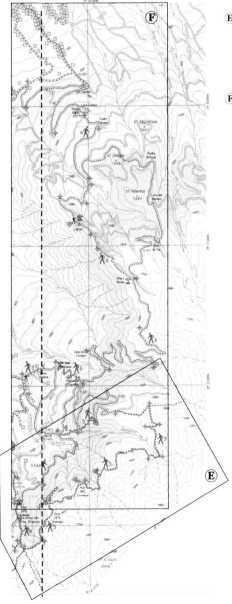

E Walk 5
  Mighty
  Mountain
  Path - Los
  Organos

F Walk 6
  King Of
  The North

N1. FLORA LOOP

The upper **Orotava Valley** is a popular region for walkers, where even on our introductory walking route we can surprise the old hands who stick to the traditional routes. These slopes are criss-crossed by walking trails and *pistas*, so it is very pleasing to find that Flora Loop covers paths not included in other walking guides. Introductory does not mean 'effortless', as in this steep landscape any circular route must involve a degree of climbing and descents. Very much a short 'forest and views' route, but not so pleasant in wet weather, for which the **Orotava Valley** is notorious!

| 3 | 1 hour | 3.8 km | 180m / 180m | 3 |

Our start point is at the **Bar/Restaurant Aguamansa (0M)** just above the bus stop, a good place for a coffee while drinking in the upper valley scenery; a contrast to the overbuilt lower valley. Across from the bar, by the 'Las Fuentes 1000m' sign, a *camino rural* (**Wp.1**) climbs up from the TF-21 main road. We steadily climb up, past the green gates (**Wp.2, 3M**) into the pine plantation, for the tarmac to level out at the gated entrance to **Granja Cinegetica Aguamansa**; a birds of prey breeding centre.

Opposite the wooden railings, a path (**Wp.3, 5M**) is signed to **La Caldera**, and taking this path, we are climbing through the green forest, passing above the chittering bird cages to a path junction (**Wp.4**, see Alternative Ascent) where we go right. We stroll along through the green wood with the TF-21 above us to come above a *pista* and a path dropping down to it (**Wp.5 and an** alternative route). Keeping straight on, we walk above the *pista* until we join it (**Wp.6, 12M**) and turn left up to the main road (**Wp.7**).

Taking care crossing the road, we stroll past the picnic area at the start of the **La Caldera** lane for 110.5 metres (just shows how accurate our mapping software is!) to take a path up into the woods on our right (**SSW, Wp.8**) signed **Camino a la Caldera**.

Alternative Ascent
When at the path junction for **Waypoint 4**, the path ahead holds the bleak prospect of the TF-21, but if you take this route you come out to a cleared area alongside the main road. Take extreme care crossing the main road to go onto a path up into the woods. Take the red earth path to the right and climb up to a surprise; on a ledge overlooking the main road is a forgotten viewpoint, **Disco Mirador**. Back in the sixties, before mass tourism, the well heeled of **Orotava** would battle up the dirt roads to park in the cleared area and then ascend to picnic at the most outstanding view of the **Orotava Valley**; much more impressive than **Mirador Humbolt** lower down the valley. Concrete seats surround a grinding wheel table with breathtaking views when the valley is clear of cloud.

After this 'lost' *mirador* - not mentioned on maps or in guide books - we continue up the path, passing a minor path off to our left, to strike the *pista* that leads to **Galería La Puente**. Turning right, we stroll along the *pista* to the **La Caldera** lane and rejoin our ascent.

Continuation
Camino a la Caldera may be signed, but due to water erosion it is a rough ascent up through the forest. Keeping to a smoother trail to the right of the eroded official route, we climb up to an area of more mature pines (**Wp.9**) where our path swings left, and the gradient moderates for us to come up to below a stone wall. Stone steps take us up to come onto the car parking area at **La Caldera** (**Wp.10, 24M**).

After the stiff climb we go left to swing past the bar (**Wp.11**, refreshment stop allowed) to leave the tarmac as we head out on the broad **Pista Monte del Pino** (**Wp.12**). It is an easy stroll down this 'Orotava walking motorway' to pass a popular walking trail crossing the *pista* (**Wp.13, 30M**) and a rough forest trail off to our right (**Wp.14**) before coming to a walking trail dropping into the forest on our left (**Wp.15, 35M**); just ahead is a *choza* and the **Chimoche** junction.

Going left, we pass a wooden spike discouraging vehicle traffic to follow the wide, boulder strewn path down into woods. Away from the crowds on this little used trail, we steadily descend through the trees, our route becoming clearer but narrower as we pass a 'sendero' marker (**Wp.16**) and a tiny path off to our right (**Wp.17**) before coming onto the *pista* serving the **Galería La Puente** (**Wp.18, 41M**). If you go left you come to the *galería* tunnel and seating area in a few metres, making for a pleasant break in this floriferous valley. Across the *pista,* our path drops down to meet it again beside a white building and a *sendero* sign (**Wp.19, 43M**).

The enormous pine at waypoint 22.

Once on the *pista*, we cross the concreted watercourse for an easy stroll up from the valley, passing a smaller *pista* off to our right (**Wp.20**) just before a major walking trail (coming down from Wp.13) crosses the dirt road (**Wp.21, 47M**). Turning right, we drop down the well-trodden path through the trees to face a simply enormous pine (**Wp.22**), just past which a trail goes left, a vandalised sign showing it as going to **Choza Dorta**. Our trail gets more water eroded before dropping us down onto the TF-21 by a *choza*-style bus stop opposite the trout farm (**Wp.23, 54M**). A relaxed stroll alongside the main road, takes us past the **Camino de Candelaria** (**Wp.24**) on our right, before arriving back at **Bar/Rest Aguamansa (60M)**.

Starting with the 345 bus to **Bar/Restaurant Aguamansa** (and the bus stop) this walk follows country lanes through lush vegetation and a couple of *barrancos*, down the eastern side of the **Orotava Valley**. The route is virtually all downhill, steep in parts but on tarmac lanes, descending from 1,050 metres to 500 metres altitude through hamlets and villages. Although downhill is not energetic, it can leave an impression on the calf muscles and knees, so treat this as a stroll and not a race. We make no excuses for this being an 'all tarmac' route as it passes through some exceptional pastoral scenery with exceptional flora.

2 | 1½ hours | 5.5 km | 50m / 620m | 3

Taking the 345 bus via the **Botanical Gardens** and **La Orotava** gives us a scenic ascent with spectacular views (sit on the right) across the **Orotava Valley**. Alighting at **Bar Aguamansa**, you might like to sample the atmosphere while taking refreshments on the bar's rustic terrace tables, from where we can soak up the views across the **Trout Farm** and pine forest and away to the mountains. Service at the bar is good, except when coach tours arrive and chaos ensues for a few minutes.

Our route starts at the bus stop (**0M**) and shelter from where we leave the main road behind as we walk steeply downhill on the small lane heading down to **El Velo**. Passing a tarmac lane on our right (**Wp.1**), two hundred metres down the lane we turn right onto the **Camino de Mamio** (**Wp.2, 3M**), the second lane we come to. In a couple of minutes we are leaving the houses behind and come into open countryside, where the fields on each side of our narrow walled lane are dotted with chestnut trees and bracken. This *camino* used to be a country track, but in recent years a tarmac lane has replaced the original donkey trail. Even so, the route retains its country charm despite the 'upgrading' for motorised traffic.

It's not long before we drop into the first of two floriferous *barrancos*. At the floor of **Barranco de los Llanos** the road forms part of the watercourse (**Wp.3**) which makes the route difficult (and not recommended) during heavy rain. Climbing out of the first *barranco*, we stroll through the pastoral countryside, passing a lane on our right (**Wp.4**) before descending into the **Barranco de la Madre**, again with the road forming part of the watercourse (**Wp.5, 15M**).

Leaving the *barrancos* behind, we come into a fertile area, lush with wild and cultivated plants. After passing a group of vegetable plots lined with fruit trees on our left, we bear left (**Wp.6**) at a junction, keeping to the 'main road' as it passes between some small cottages and dry stone walls dotted with ferns. Down the country lane we come to the meeting of the **Mamio/Pinoleris/La Florida** lanes (**Wp.7, 27M** and sign posted and with a shrine on the corner). Our 'Classic Choza' walk joins us from the **Perez Ventoza** lane, as we keep left at the junction and continue gently downhill on the narrow lane.

We are now getting well into the walk, passing a track on our right (**Wp.8**) and need to keep a sharp lookout for house Nº 68, **La Zaraza** (**Wp.9**), on our right - it is easy to walk past this house without noticing. Immediately past the house is a junction (**Wp.10**) where we turn right onto the small lane of **Los Caminos**.

If you miss this junction then continuing straight ahead on the main lane after **La Zaraza** would take us downhill to drop down through a steep and tight s-bend and into a *barranco*. Crossing the *barranco* on a small white bridge, we pass a shrine before coming into countryside similar to our main route but without the views. Continuing downhill the incorrect route is confirmed when we find ourselves overlooking the main road at a hairpin bend by the **La Curva Bar** and K9 marker. If you find yourself in this position you can easily rejoin our 'correct' route by taking the street heading east (**E**) from the bar. Keep on the street and in just under a kilometre you will meet the correct route at a junction with a yellow sign for **La Florida & Pinoleris**.

Back on the small lane just after **La Zaraza**, we stroll down through a quiet countryside of trees and stone walls. Densely growing foliage allows only occasional glimpses of the houses set back from the narrow lane, such as **Finca El Bosque (Wp.11)**. As we continue downhill, the dense foliage gives way to vegetable plots and houses, allowing us extensive views over the eastern part of the **Orotava Valley**, as we come down to a t-junction marked by a bent 'Stop' sign (**Wp.12, 47M**), and here we turn left.

Sand coloured walls topped with geraniums line the right side of the road and we are soon passing a large picnic area and a church on our left as we come down to another road junction (**Wp.13**). The street from **La Curva Bar** joins us from the left as we keep right to follow the yellow **La Florida & Pinoleris** sign. We are now passing through a grape area with vines covering the terraces, occasionally interspersed with vegetable plots. Far ahead the small village of **Pino Alto** can be seen clinging high up on the edge of the cliffs which form the valley wall.

As well as enjoying the views, keep an eye open for an excellent example of a Canarian thatched hut with its eaves brushing the ground (**Wp.14**), while behind it dramatic pine forested mountain slopes rise steeply. Keeping to the main lane we come to another road junction where the **Bar Florida Alto** (**Wp.15, 62M**) announces the high part of **La Florida**. Following the road round to the right, our route ahead drops steeply downhill in a straight line between tightly packed two storey houses decorated with flowering plants on the edges of their flat roofs. The end of the hill is marked by a church and school on our right (**Wp.16**), just before we come to the cross-roads in **La Florida** (**Wp.17, 77M**) with the narrow lane to **Pino Alto** dropping into the valley on our right.

A comfortable urban *choza* beside the crossroads is a good place to enjoy the views and take a couple of minutes to decide what to do next. We have walked nearly five kilometres, and while the downhill route isn't very strenuous it can be hard on the legs. From where we stand the *camino rural* to **Pino Alto** drops to our right before climbing steeply (100 metres) into the village. Our choice is to turn left and seek refreshment in the appropriately named **Bar La Tranquilidad**. Suitably refreshed, you could wait for the La Florida - La Orotava bus (hourly), but far better to walk off that food by strolling through this affluent village, dropping into and climbing out of yet another *barranco* (look for the pedestrian stairs), to meet the main road and wait for the regular and frequent bus service back to **Puerto de la Cruz**.

N3. CHOZA CLASSIC

If one route characterised walking in the **Orotava Valley**, then it would have to be the **Choza Perez Ventoso** 'Choza Classic'. Bus riders will have the advantage over car drivers by starting at **La Caldera** but having the option to finish downhill to **La Florida** or **El Bebedero**; a far easier finish than the stiff climb up through **Aguamansa** to **La Caldera**. Easy route finding combines with good scenery and bucolic charm to create the valley's most popular walking route.

In wet weather the steep path down the valley wall from **Choza El Topo** becomes very slippery indeed. If you get caught in wet weather - not unusual in the **Orotava Valley** - then descend on the shortest alternative route by going down the *pista* signed to **Aguamansa** - see map.

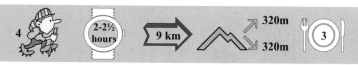

4 | 2-2½ hours | 9 km | 320m / 320m | 3

Montaña Teide in the distance as seen from Pista Monte del Pino.

We start out from the **La Caldera** car park and bus stop (**Wp.1, 0M**) to stroll past the bar and out onto the **Pista Monte del Pino** (**Wp.2**). Down past the trail of our return route (**Wp.32**), and our 'Flora Loop' path (**Wp.3**), we pass the *choza* at the **Chimoche/Pedro Gil** path junction (**10M**) to continue along the broad *pista*; GPS users will find it best to walk on the left of the *pista* to reduce the effect of 'mountain shadowing' caused by the steep valley wall on our right.

Our route curves into and out of a small *barranco* before we come to impressively balanced giant rocks (**Wp.4**) opposite a chained off private *pista*. **Pista Monte del Pino** now meanders along going gently downhill, with only occasional views through the trees, for us to pass a little-used path on our left (**Wp.5**) before swinging down to round an impressive stone house (**Wp.6, 28M**) sitting just above the **Barranco de la Madre**'s watercourse.

Over the *barranco*'s bridged watercourse, our route starts to climb steadily, water eroded in places, with the valley steepening on our left. Curving up to leave the valley behind, we come to the **Aguamansa** *pista* (**Wp.7, 35M**) signed off to our left; if you opt for this alternative you are now at the highest point of your route. We continue up the **Pista Monte del Pino**, steadily climbing until the *pista* reaches a crest (**Wp.8**) where after a flat section we are

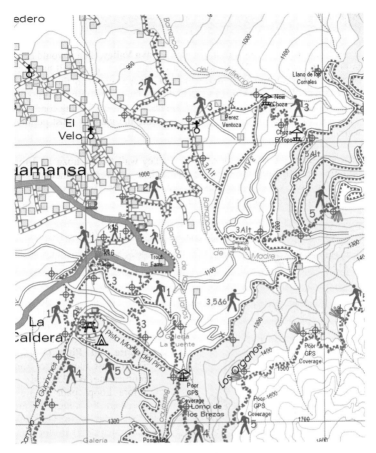

climbing again. It is a steady uphill, accompanied by impressive glimpses through the trees, all the way up to **Choza El Topo** (**Wp.9, 45M**) with its *pista* and path cross-roads. At the *choza*, a broad *pista* climbs up to the right, an alternative **Los Organos** route, while **Pista Monte del Pino** continues ahead and a path drops down beside the *choza*. **Choza El Topo** is a popular 'motorway' rest point and you will be lucky to find the seats unoccupied.

From **Choza El Topo** we take the path dropping steeply down the forested slopes. The path starts steeply and gets steeper as we skitter down through a series of zigzags to a *pista* going left off a hairpin bend (**Wp.10, 51M**). By now you will see why we do not recommend this route in wet weather, when you are likely to slither down out of control to arrive at the bottom looking like a pig in the proverbial. More steep zigzags down past a *sendero* sign (**Wp.11**) bring us down alongside a *choza* perched above the path on our right, just as we meet the **Aguamansa** *pista* (**Wp.12, 60M**). This is the **New Choza** which most people imagine to be **Choza Perez Ventoso**, and you should find space on its benches but unfortunately the table has been stolen!

From **New Choza** we continue downhill on the wide *pista* to a beautiful view of **Montaña Teide** framed by the tall trees (**Wp.13**) before dropping down to the **Perez Ventoso** marker (**Wp.14**). On the opposite side of the *pista* you can see the few remains of the base of **Choza Perez Ventoso** but the wooden structure finally rotted away in 1995, though it is still shown on some maps.

Now we come onto a narrow *camino rural* which takes us out into a bucolic landscape of farm plots and log cabins, enhanced by the flowers and white broom lining the narrow lane. Passing a concrete lane on our left (**Wp.15**) we stroll along to the shrine junction with our 'Downhill to La Florida' route (**Wp.16, 69M**). Here bus riders can opt for an easy finish by going right, while we turn uphill for a steady climb up past houses to a junction (**Wp.17**) where our 'wet weather' alternative (signed 'Organos de Piedra Aventura') comes down the concrete lane to join us.

Keeping to the tarmac lane (signed 'Aguamansa'), we stroll past a dirt lane (**Wp.18**) to drop into **Barranco de la Madre**, and then it is up to pass a concrete lane on our left (**Wp.19**) before dropping into the **Barranco de los Llanos**. Taking a walking trail (**Wps. 20 & 21**) we cut off a loop of the lane and then climbing up the lane out of the *barranco*. Now it is easy strolling along the lane past the first houses to meet the **El Velo** street at the **Camino de Mamio** street sign (**Wp.22, 85M**).

Now it is seriously uphill as we turn left to climb up the steep street to come onto the TF-21 by the bus stop (**Wp.23, 90M**). Going left, we walk up to the **Bar/Rest Aguamansa** and give in to the temptation for refreshments before tackling the climb up to **La Caldera**.

From the bar (**0M**) we cross the TF-21 to take the 'Flora Loop' *camino rural* up to the 'La Caldera' signed path (**Wp.24**). Climbing up through the woods, we keep straight on at the path junction (**Wp.25**) to climb up to the TF-21 (**6M**). Carefully crossing the road, we take the path into the woods. Keeping right on the red earth path we climb up through the woods to a surprise; the little-known **Disco Mirador** (**Wp.26**) complete with seats and 'grinding wheel' table, not to mention an awesome view of the **Orotava Valley** when it is not cloudy. Back on our path, we climb up through the trees, passing a smoother path off to our left (**Wp.27**) before emerging onto the **Galería La Puente** *pista* (**Wp.28**).

Once on the *pista*, the shortest route is to go right to the **La Caldera** access road and then take the 'Flora Loop' path for a stiff climb up through the trees to the **La Caldera** car park. We opt to go left for a gentle stroll down to where a major walking trail crosses the *pista* (**Wp.29**). Here we turn right to follow the broad path up through the woods in lazy zigzags, passing *sendero* signs (**Wps. 30 & 31**) before emerging onto the **Pista Monte del Pino** (**Wp.32, 31M**). Going right, it is a gentle uphill stroll, retracing our outward route back past the bar to the car park.

4. CHIMOCHE LOOP

An easy tour of the upper **Orotava Valley**, taking in sections of classic walking trails before descending back to **La Caldera** by a little-known walking trail. Take your time on the strenuous climb up through the forest on the **Candelaria Trail** and you will be rewarded with easy strolling to **Choza Chimoche** plus a relaxed descent back to your start point. Should you be caught out by bad weather, or find the climb too much, there are three options to shorten this route.

3   2 hours   6 km   240m / 240m   2*

*Refreshments at **La Caldera**

We start out from the parking area at **La Caldera** (**Wp.1, 0M**) to stroll past the bar and round to the junction with the main *pista forestal* (**Wp.2**) signed **Los Organos**. It is an easy stroll down the broad *pista* passing a water pipeline (**Wp.3**) and a walking trail crossing our route (**Wp.4**). Over a bridge, we pass a track off to our right (**Wp.5**) to come to a *pista* off to the left (**Wp.6**) just before the *choza* and *fuente* at the 'Pedro Gil, Chimoche' junction (**Wp.7, 10M**). Here we leave the *pista* to follow the clear, signed path up into the forest.

Now it is across a watercourse, and then we are into a relentless ascent through the pines and tree heather, gentle at first as we come up to pass the three crosses (**Wp.8, 12M**) but then getting steeper as we zigzag up the valley wall. You'll need a top-notch GPS unit to keep satellite signals amongst all these trees and the steep valley wall, not that there is any danger of getting lost as there is just one clear path and we are on it.

Taking breaks whenever we need them, we gradually ascend up through the twists and turns to come to a clearer area by some large eucalyptus trees (**Wp.9**) and a shrine set in the crook of a hairpin bend (**Wp.10**). Just a little more climbing brings us up onto a *pista forestal* at **Lomo de los Brezos** (**Wp.11, 25M**) for a welcome break. You can shortcut the route at this point by going right on the *pista* and at a T-junction go right again to head down to **La Caldera**.

Across the *pista* from the **Lomo de los Brezos** sign, we go up onto a small walking trail which winds up amongst the trees in a series of zigzags. The trees are less dense than lower down, allowing good GPS reception. As usual it is onwards and upwards on the relentless ascent, taking breaks whenever you need them, the magnificent **Los Organos** cliffs glimpsed through the trees on our left providing some light relief. There is so little to comment on in this bland section of forest that even a small rock outcrop (**Wp.12**) seems like a major feature before we come up to a junction (**Wp.13, 40M**). Here a broad earth path sweeps gently down into the valley on our right, our second opportunity to short cut.

Spurning temptation, we continue uphill through the thinning pines to climb

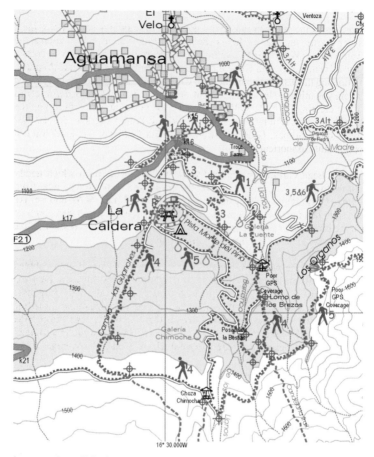

into a region of black *picon* where our path goes up through a narrow trench (**Wp.14**) before coming to a T-junction (**Wp.15, 45M**). Here the **Los Organos** path comes in from the left; definitely not a short cut!

We go right to continue up to come below a huge Canarian pine with a large red arrow sprayed on its trunk (**Wp.16, 47M**). Don't worry - the upward route signed by the arrow is the **Candelaria** pilgrimage route, and we are now at the top of our relentless ascent as we pass the pilgrimage path on our left to stroll along above a tree filled ravine.

Our path undulates along to cross a picturesque rocky watercourse (**Wp.17, 50M**) before climbing quite steeply to come above a sheer ravine, *Aeonium canariensis* and other 'rock roses' of the Crassula family lining the small cliff on our left before heading across the ravines watercourse below a floriferous cliff (**Wp.18**).

'rock roses'

Now our route starts to run gently downhill as it swings south alongside a sheer ravine, unusual as this is sheer earth rather than rock. Crossing the watercourse (**Wp.19, 56M**) we round a ridge into a gentler valley to cross a pair of watercourses to come onto the end of a dirt *pista forestal* (**Wp.20**). Following the *pista* we come along to **Choza Chimoche**, an often busy *choza* where you might be lucky to get a seat, at a junction of *pistas forestales* set in a forest clearing (**Wp.21, 59M**). From the *choza* you can go north (**N**) on the right hand *pista*, the favoured route of most walking writers, to descend the broad dirt road past **Galería Chimoche** to **La Caldera**; our third and last opportunity to shortcut.

From **Choza Chimoche** we head west (**W**) along the pista which gently climbs to give occasional views over the trees to the ocean. Ten minutes from **Choza Chimoche** a walking trail crosses the *pista* (**Wp.22, 68M**) and we take the right hand path. Although this junction is marked by small signs high up on the pine trees, 'La Caldera' right and 'M. Limon' left, it is easily missed, and the next junction is at the TF-21 main road!

Stepping off the *pista*, we come down into the green wood on a cobbled donkey trail, unfortunately littered with stones making for slow progress along to cross a watercourse (**Wp.23**). Although technically part of the same forest this is a softer, greener woodland compared to the harsh pines and tree heather on the ascent up the **Pedro Gil** path. Our trail twists down through the trees in a steady descent, the trees closing over our route to form a green tunnel (**Wp.24, 77M**); despite the tree cover we still have good GPS coverage.

After the green tunnel the woodland opens up (**Wp.25**) as we cross a small watercourse, and the path is less rock littered. Continuously descending, the path stone littered again, we come down to cross a water pipeline (**Wp.26, 92M**) and the woodland opens out around our route for a short section (**Wp.27**). Laurel trees supplement the Canarian pines and tree heathers as we continue down alongside moss covered rocks to come to the end of the *sendero*, signed on a large pine, at a dirt *pista* (**Wp.28, 102M**). Going left, we come down the rocky *pista* to the **Caldera** road (**Wp.29**), the *pista* signed 'Camino de los Guanches', to cross straight over onto a woodland path which takes us through the wood, passing a path off to our right (**Wp.30**) before coming down onto the tarmac again at the parking area (**105M** continuous walking).

N5. MIGHTY MOUNTAIN PATH - LOS ORGANOS

Northern Tenerife has one true classic walk, and this is it. Following an amazing woodland and ravine trail, we traverse the south-east wall of the **Orotava Valley**, taking in a surfeit of scenery, views, flora and orogenical geology. You need good weather and an adequate fitness level, but if you have these, then this is one route not to miss.

Some walkers are discouraged from this route by the 'alarmingly vertiginous' description given in some guide books, but as vertigo sufferers we found no problems. There is a very short exposed stretch but even here a well fixed steel-pipe handrail gives confidence. Those 'other guide books' give very curt descriptions for this route, and some of the few items they mention (guard rails at a viewpoint, Wp.50) disappeared years ago, so we take their 'vertiginous' warnings as being equally up to date.

*Catering at La Caldera

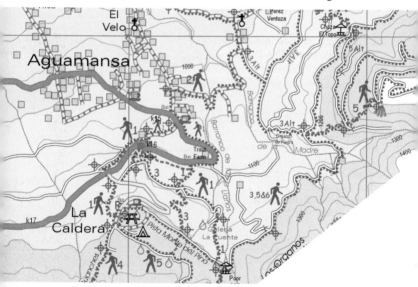

We start from the **La Caldera** car park (**Wp.1, 0M**) following the road past the bar and out onto the **Pista Monte del Pino**, passing the *choza* at the **Chimoche** path junction (**Wp.2, 8M**). You probably know this stretch of walking 'motorway' as well as your footwear as we pass the balanced rocks and private *pista* (**Wp.3, 15M**) before dropping down past the stone house to cross the stone bridge (**Wp.4, 27M**) and labouring up the steady ascent to the

Aguamansa signed *pista* (**Wp.5, 30M**); which seemed quick today.

Now the path finding and the exertions begin. Ten metres past the *pista* a faint, easily missed, dirt path climbs up into the forest (**Wp.6**). The path is poorly defined in places, a couple of small cairns providing guidance (**Wps. 7 to 13** provide waypoint navigation for this section) in deciding which is path and which is water runoff, as we climb steeply up through the pines and tree heather in a 'puff and grunt' ascent to a large pine whose roots make steps in the path (**Wp.14**). From the large pine, we climb up steeply through hairpin bends (**Wps. 15 & 16**) before emerging onto the broad *pista* coming up from **Choza El Topo** (**Wp.17, 47M**). If walking the route in reverse, we recommend using the *pista* rather than the steep woodland paths.

Going right we go onto another faint path (**Wp.18**) which climbs up from the *pista* junction. Again it is steeply up through the pines and heather, another 'puff and grunt' ascent (**Wps. 19, 20 & 21**) brings us up to a small clearing (**Wp.22, 57M**) amongst the mature pines with comfortable rocks. From the clearing our path seems to get even steeper (**Wps. 23 & 24**) as we labour up to climb onto the *pista* again (**Wp.25, 68M**).

After the steep ascents the *pista* makes for a relaxed stroll, and in a couple of minutes we come to a 'seat height' rock with panoramic views of **Teide** (**Wp.26, 70M**). An easy stroll takes us up the *pista* to its crest (**Wp.27**), and even a gentle downhill before coming to the rock arrow (**Wp.28, 82M**) pointing us off the *pista* onto the **Organos** path.

We are amongst mature pines, soon climbing steeply again (**Wp.29**) before coming onto a broad *lomo*. After the gentle *lomo* we are back to a 'puff and grunt' steep climb going up through zigzags (**Wp.31**) to a long climbing traverse (**Wp.32**) which brings us out of the trees to a 'rock gate' (**Wp.33, 100M**). Just above the 'rock gate' we come to a junction (**Wp.34**) with green arrow waymarking. Going right, we are immediately rewarded with a pleasant woodland path which contours along with magnificent views before starting to descend below a cliff (poor GPS reception) to a hairpin bend (**Wp.35**). Our path drops down through another hairpin (**Wp.36**) before our steep descent runs out (**Wp.37**) for us to cross a water runoff (**Wp.38, 118M**) with good views down over the **Orotava Valley**.

Our route now climbs up around a spur in the valley wall and then undulates along before dropping down into a sharp ravine, crossing the ravines two watercourses

At the rock viewpoint, 155 minutes into the walk.

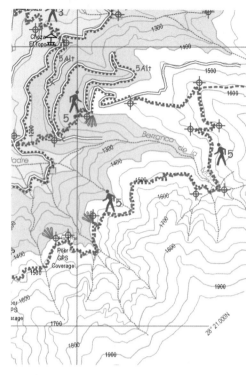

(**Wps. 39** & **40**), our voices echoing in this beautiful orogenical landscape. We turn into another ravine, dropping down to cross its watercourse (**Wp.41**) and climbing out to come into a most unusual ravine with a 'rock boulder river' (**Wp.42, 130M**) falling from the heights above us steeply down the valley wall.

The steep valley of **Barranco de la Madre** widens out as we meander along a steady ascent, curving left to resume progress along the valley wall. A fallen pine (**Wp.43**) is easily negotiated just before we zigzag up to a higher level to continue westwards (**W**). We continue ascending past a second fallen pine, the high altitude woodland and ravine path having some areas of unprotected drops, but not seriously vertiginous so far.

After swinging south (**S**), we drop down to cross another steep ravine (**Wp.44**) and another climb before our path starts descending through hairpin bends (**Wp.45**) in lazy zigzags to bring us down to a rock viewpoint overlooking **Aguamansa** (**Wp.46, 155M**).

From the *mirador*, we continue downhill on the rock and shale surface to turn into a pocket in the valley wall where we come below a huge knob of rock. We cross the cutting's first watercourse by a pair of boulders (**Wp.47**) and then cross the second watercourse directly beneath the huge knob of rock. Due to the orogenical landscape as our path climbs beneath steep cliffs we lose GPS coverage in this section of the route. Now we have tree heathers on our right, creating a green tunnel effect until we come to face the vertiginous section.

A rock ledge curves out of sight beneath overhanging cliffs (**Wp.48**), but don't worry. A securely fixed steel pipe provides a hand rail as we edge round into the unknown above a precipitous drop. Just round the corner we step off the ledge back onto a normal width path and regain GPS coverage (**Wp.49**) for a short climb up to *mirador* viewpoint (**Wp.50, 170M**) on a rock promontory; the guard rails referred to in some 'guidebooks' rotted away over ten years ago!

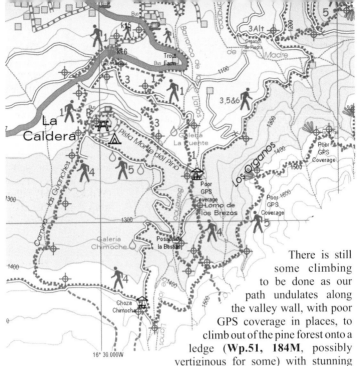

There is still some climbing to be done as our path undulates along the valley wall, with poor GPS coverage in places, to climb out of the pine forest onto a ledge (**Wp.51, 184M**, possibly vertiginous for some) with stunning views in good weather. Further on we pass an rock outcrop (**Wp.52**) providing another viewpoint over the valley before turning down into a ravine, the trees clearing again for more views (**Wp.53**) after which the path becomes a rough rocky descent of long lazy zigzags to cross a ravine's watercourse (**Wp.54, 202M**).

In the next ravine (**Wp.55**) three steep valleys meet, each stuffed with endemic trees and plants, unusual in this rocky landscape. Just past the ravine we loose GPS coverage as we come to face a long slope. Trudging up the steep incline we finally arrive at the junction with our 'Chimoche Loop' route (**Wp.56, 215M**) and can swing downhill on the grit trail to a path junction (**Wp.57, 222M**).

You could continue straight down to **Lomo de los Brezos** but we are looking for a less skittery descent, so we go left at the junction to descend on a gentle woodland trail above a gentler valley, when compared to the orogenical landscape earlier. Coming to a junction (**Wp.58**) we take the lower path to the right which winds down through the woods, our path becoming more trench-like as we descend before we drop down onto a dirt *pista* (**Wp.59, 233M**). **Lomo de los Brezos** is to the right as we go left to climb up to the junction at **Pasada de los Bestias**.

Keeping straight ahead, we are on the *pista* which descends from **Choza Chimoche**, unremarkable except that we have a fast, easy walking descent through the forest down to cross the **Caldera** ring road (**Wp.61, 252M**). Across the tarmac to follow the path through the woods, and we are stepping down onto the end of the **La Caldera** car park at **254M**; actual walking time excluding breaks.

N6. KING OF THE NORTH

If you enjoy all day walks on country lanes, then this is the route for you. We walk on good *pistas forestales* with our finishes on narrow *camino rural* tarmac lanes. Originally we finished in **Santa Ursula**, but not everyone wants to go to **Santa Ursula** so we have an alternative ending passing through **Pino Alto** to finish at **La Florida**. *Pistas* are technically public rights of way, but more locked gates are appearing on private dirt roads, which look exactly like *pistas forestales*. Private landowners are becoming much more protective of access to their land so that you could well find old walk descriptions of this region which use farm tracks and paths are now impassable.

Grab an early bus up to **La Caldera**, pack plenty of refreshment and wet weather gear in case the weather changes, and enjoy a grand tour of the forest and farmland which makes up the eastern **Orotava Valley**.

4	5½ hours	21 km	400m / 1000m	0

Starting from the **La Caldera** car park and bus stop (**Wp.1, 0M**) we stroll out past the bar and onto the **Pista Monte del Pino**. Keeping to this 'walking motorway' that we know so well, we climb up to the **Choza El Topo** (**Wp.2, 45M**) and its path and *pistas* junction.

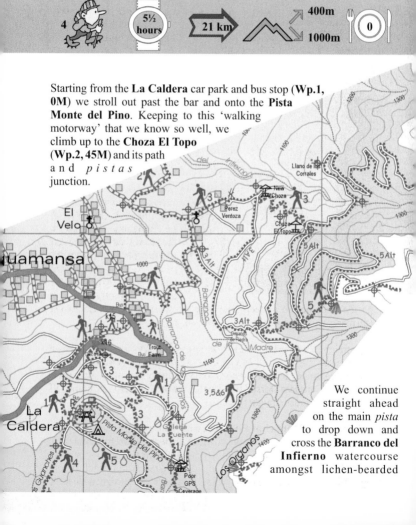

We continue straight ahead on the main *pista* to drop down and cross the **Barranco del Infierno** watercourse amongst lichen-bearded trees (**Wp.3**). Now it is steadily uphill between the cliffs and the ravine to come up to the **Llano de los Corrales** plinth (**Wp.4**) and a path dropping down into the valley. Our route turns away from the steep *barranco* ravine in a steady and seemingly relentless ascent, scaling the eastern valley wall in a series of hairpin bends. A large stone cairn (**Wp.5**) shows we are well into the climb with only two more major hairpins before we reach the *pista*'s crest (**Wp.6**) where it runs through a rock cutting.

Already that is a lot of walking, and not a little climbing, relieved by the panoramic views seen through the gaps in the trees. Now we have an easier time as we climb up to the **Choza Almadi** junction (**Wp.7, 169M**). The rebuilt *choza* sits below the junction making for a pleasant rest and recovery stopping place. From **Choza Almadi** we have a choice of routes; 'Original' and 'New Las Lajitas'.

Original DWG Route

Keeping to the main *pista*, signed to **Corujera** and **Santa Ursula**, we drop down northwards (**N**) in a gentle descent through the forest with occasional yellow diamond *sendero* signs nailed to trees. A kilometre on, we come to the **Cruz de Tea** marker plinth where we ignore the *pista* going left into the valley and keep to the main *pista* to gently descend through the trees before a steeper descent brings us down to **Lomo del Barreno** marker plinth at a major *pista* junction.

We keep straight ahead on the **Monte de Santa Ursula** *pista* to drop down past the municipal boundary 'T.M.La Orotava'. At the next junction, **Piedra del Agua** we continue on the main *pista* to come down to a major junction at **Los Assientos**, 'Carretera Dorsal' is off to the right and 'Morro Los Pinos' off to the left, while we cross straight over.

At the next junction, **Morro Los Pinos** and with 'Morro Los Pinos' signed on the *pista* to the left, we again continue on the main *pista* signed for 'Pino Alto, Santa Ursula, La Orotava'; some of these *pistas* are as well signed as the main roads. Gently descending, we pass an unsigned *pista* off to our left before arriving at **Montañas de las Ovejas** where 'Las Arenitas' is signed back the

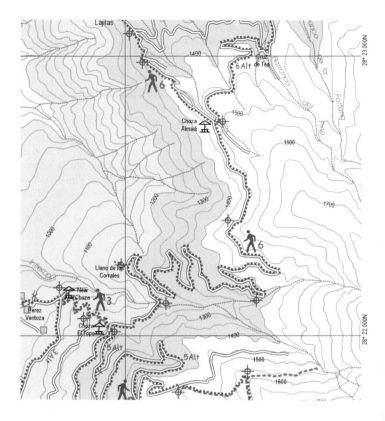

way we have come. Staying on the main *pista* we come down to a junction at **Coral de Gabmorra**, and ignoring the 'sin salida' *pista* we continue down past the **Jueves de la Cueva** name marker, and a trail signed to 'Zona Recreativa', before we come down to join our new route. This is pleasant strolling route in good weather, but our new route from **Choza Almadi** is both more spectacular and shorter.

New DWG Las Lajitas Route

At **Choza Almadi**, we leave the **Pista Monte del Pino** by going left on the broad *pista* heading north west. Soon the *pista* divides (**Wp.8**), going straight ahead on the smaller *pista* takes us up for views over the valley before dropping down to rejoin the main *pista* (**Wp.9**) again. We drop down passing minor *pistas* off to our right (**Wps. 10 & 11**) before our route runs out onto a broad *lomo* at **Las Lajitas** (**Wp.12**) where, from the cross, we have one of the best views of the **Orotava Valley**. There is also an undamaged *choza* opposite the cross, so if **Choza Almadi** is full, you could postpone lunch until reaching **Las Lajitas**.

Below **Las Lajitas** a recently bulldozed *pista* has eliminated the paths referred to in some walking guides, confusing some walkers. We drop down the *pista*, very slippery if wet, to pass a minor *pista* off to our right (**Wp.13**) before coming to another junction (**Wp.14**) where we go right.

We have come down into one of the pockets of the original laurel forest (**Wp.15**) as we stroll beneath the dark green leaf canopy with rods of sunlight penetrating the thick woods. As we come out of the laurels we face a confusing T-junction (**Wp.16**) where **Pino Alto** is signed both left and right. We go right to cross the municipal boundary (**Wp.17**) and come to a T-junction (**Wp.18, 228M**) where our original route joins us from the **Pino de las Nigeres** *pista* coming into the junction from the right.

We leave the junction on the P. **Hoya la Mora** *pista* for a gentle downhill stroll which brings us down to **Cuatro Caminos** name marker (**Wp.19**) at another major *pista* crossroads. Taking the **Pino Alto**, **La Orotava**, **Santa Ursula** *pista* we continue down through the forest to the next junction (**Wp.20**) where a *pista* is signed left as 'Pista La Orotava'; don't believe this sign, as going left here would just take you back in a loop to the two 'Pino Alto' signs junction (Wp.16).

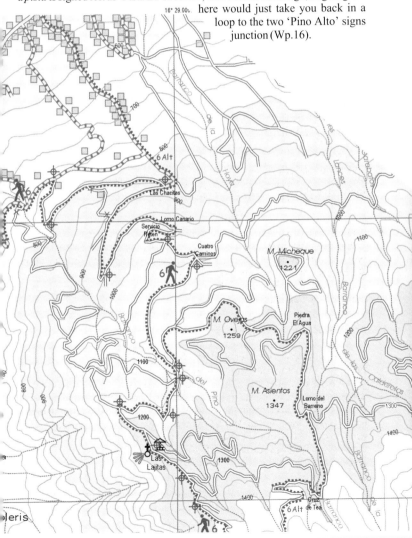

Keeping right, our route now curves right below the trees, with tree heather on our left, for us to come along to **Lomo el Canario (Wp.21)** and the junior sized shelter, table and benches signed **Servicio Reten Incendio**. Our *pista* curves left, giving glimpses of farm land as we pass a donkey trail on our right **(Wp.22)** to come to views down over farm plots to the north coast with its breeze block townships. Our *pista* turns sharp right **(N, Wp.23)** with a minor *pista* off to the left and we pass two more *pistas* off to our left **(Wps. 24 & 25)** before coming down to **Las Charquitas (Wp.26, 277M)** for a choice between **Santa Ursula** and **Pino Alto** routes.

Santa Ursula finish

At **Las Charquitas** continue straight ahead onto the tarmac lane. This *camino rural* turns left and then heads directly down in a steep descent past farm plots and small settlements, starting at number 67 where the lane gets even steeper. A final very steep section drops us down onto a T-junction on **La Corujera's** 'main road'.

We go left and first right to continue the steep descent past **Bar Casa Fefe**, taking the pedestrian street **Calle Los Quartos** as a short break from the traffic. It is all steeply down, taking a staired pedestrian path, before dropping onto the main road on the western outskirts of **Santa Ursula**. From here you could stroll into the centre of the town for refreshment, or wait at the first bus stop for the frequent bus service to **La Orotava** and **Puerto de la Cruz**.

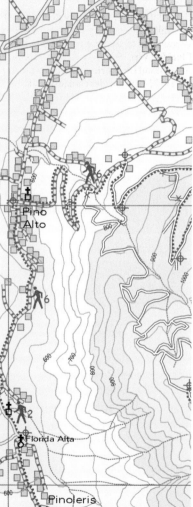

New finish to La Florida via Pino Alto

At **Las Charquitas** we turn left onto the **Pista Rosade Aguila** which heads westwards. It is a rough, little used *pista* that steadily descends past a barred *pista* on the left (**Wp.27**) before dropping more steeply to a T-junction (**Wp.28**) where we go right on a more comfortable *pista* surface.

Our *pista* curves right for us to come onto tarmac by a house (**Wp.29**) just before a T-junction (**Wp.30**). Turning left we simply stay on the main lane as it drops down the steep valley wall in a large zigzag before running out past **Pino Alto** church (**Wp.31**) to a T-Junction (**Wp.32, 327M**).

Going left we have a skittery steep descent down past the houses of **Pino Alto**, the walking becoming easier as we leave the houses behind and cross the valley floor to face the climb up to the crossroads and 'urban choza' in **La Florida** (**Wp.33**). You could wait for the bus here, or go right and follow the street round **La Florida** and across the **Barranco de Quinquita** to climb up to the TF-21 with a wider choice of buses (**370M**).

See the notes on GPS use and waypoints in the introduction on page 11.

N1.
FLORA LOOP

Wp	N	W
1	28 21.674	16 29.806
2	28 21.644	16 29.878
3	28 21.640	16 29.923
4	28 21.623	16 29.917
5	28 21.589	16 29.995
6	28 21.514	16 30.119
7	28 21.506	16 30.101
8	28 21.470	16 30.046
9	28 21.368	16 30.071
10	28 21.354	16 30.043
11	28 21.389	16 29.996
12	28 21.376	16 29.942
13	28 21.286	16 29.780
14	28 21.246	16 29.721
15	28 21.179	16 29.627
16	28 21.331	16 29.634
17	28 21.347	16 29.624
18	28 21.359	16 29.626
19	28 21.379	16 29.633
20	28 21.436	16 29.744
21	28 21.458	16 29.783
22	28 21.517	16 29.741
23	28 21.550	16 29.692
24	28 21.561	16 29.650

N2.
DOWN TO LA FLORIDA

Wp	N	W
1	28 21.749	16 29.821
2	28 21.822	16 29.821
3	28 21.753	16 29.674
4	28 21.811	16 29.625
5	28 21.821	16 29.530
6	28 21.953	16 29.537
7	28 22.052	16 29.563
8	28 22.081	16 29.624
9	28 22.107	16 29.802
10	28 22.119	16 29.812
11	28 22.359	16 29.716
12	28 22.613	16 29.798
13	28 22.663	16 29.875
14	28 22.749	16 29.928
15	28 22.950	16 29.902
16	28 23.268	16 30.032
17	28 23.318	16 30.055

N3.
CHOZA CLASSIC

Wp	N	W
1	28 21.383	16 30.035
2	28 21.370	16 29.930
3	28 21.179	16 29.616
4	28 21.319	16 29.408
5	28 21.540	16 29.168
6	28 21.571	16 29.129
7	28 21.648	16 29.273
8	28 21.782	16 29.217
9	28 22.042	16 29.072
10	28 22.065	16 29.165
11	28 22.104	16 29.186
12	28 22.143	16 29.280
13	28 22.131	16 29.305
14	28 22.109	16 29.382
15	28 22.092	16 29.490
16	28 22.055	16 29.564
17	28 21.956	16 29.533
18	28 21.893	16 29.567
19	28 21.818	16 29.624
20	28 21.787	16 29.665
21	28 21.773	16 29.678
22	28 21.827	16 29.819
23	28 21.719	16 29.820
24	28 21.644	16 29.923
25	28 21.630	16 29.913
26	28 21.603	16 29.950
27	28 21.577	16 29.977
28	28 21.560	16 29.983
29	28 21.454	16 29.801
30	28 21.398	16 29.804
31	28 21.357	16 29.770
32	28 21.301	16 29.779

N4.
CHIMOCHE LOOP

Wp	N	W
1	28 21.388	16 30.025
2	28 21.376	16 29.936
3	28 21.320	16 29.834
4	28 21.286	16 29.782
5	28 21.252	16 29.722
6	28 21.189	16 29.621
7	28 21.181	16 29.618
8	28 21.152	16 29.607
9	28 21.070	16 29.618
10	28 21.066	16 29.615
11	28 21.058	16 29.610

N5.
LOS ORGANOS

Wp	N	W
1	28 21.386	16 30.025
2	28 21.184	16 29.620
3	28 21.311	16 29.411
4	28 21.576	16 29.122
5	28 21.644	16 29.276
6	28 21.658	16 29.266
7	28 21.640	16 29.252
8	28 21.644	16 29.245
9	28 21.650	16 29.217
10	28 21.643	16 29.209
11	28 21.651	16 29.189
12	28 21.657	16 29.176
13	28 21.686	16 29.164
14	28 21.681	16 29.159
15	28 21.688	16 29.147
16	28 21.684	16 29.136
17	28 21.702	16 29.101
18	28 21.696	16 29.088
19	28 21.697	16 29.080
20	28 21.701	16 29.071
21	28 21.713	16 29.047
22	28 21.722	16 29.030
23	28 21.746	16 29.015
24	28 21.761	16 28.996
25	28 21.782	16 28.970
26	28 21.765	16 28.959
27	28 21.809	16 28.916

The following waypoints (12–30) continue the CHOZA CLASSIC list in the right column:

Wp	N	W
12	28 20.945	16 29.570
13	28 20.904	16 29.591
14	28 20.839	16 29.569
15	28 20.831	16 29.558
16	28 20.821	16 29.576
17	28 20.719	16 29.621
18	28 20.681	16 29.668
19	28 20.656	16 29.761
20	28 20.634	16 29.786
21	28 20.694	16 29.831
22	28 20.773	16 30.148
23	28 20.786	16 30.245
24	28 20.854	16 30.278
25	28 20.912	16 30.245
26	28 21.056	16 30.188
27	28 21.080	16 30.170
28	28 21.241	16 30.091
29	28 21.305	16 30.055
30	28 21.337	16 30.043

Wp	N	W
28	28 21.811	16 28.781
29	28 21.803	16 28.702
30	28 21.788	16 28.620
31	28 21.786	16 28.555
32	28 21.834	16 28.511
33	28 21.851	16 28.502
34	28 21.848	16 28.494
35	28 21.709	16 28.420
36	28 21.704	16 28.498
37	28 21.689	16 28.450
38	28 21.641	16 28.429
39	28 21.497	16 28.415
40	28 21.483	16 28.402
41	28 21.479	16 28.443
42	28 21.497	16 28.495
43	28 21.541	16 28.618
44	28 21.411	16 28.780
45	28 21.353	16 28.902
46	28 21.366	16 28.924
47	28 21.271	16 28.922
48	28 21.299	16 29.023
49	28 21.309	16 29.018
50	28 21.298	16 29.072
51	28 21.165	16 29.270
52	28 21.158	16 29.330
53	28 21.072	16 29.325
54	28 21.005	16 29.374
55	28 20.882	16 29.399
56	28 20.826	16 29.540
57	28 20.905	16 29.584
58	28 20.851	16 29.635
59	28 20.930	16 29.702
60	28 20.954	16 29.733
61	28 21.317	16 30.036

N6.

KING OF THE NORTH

Wp	N	W
1	28 21.383	16 30.035
2	28 22.042	16 29.072
3	28 22.122	16 28.858
4	28 22.244	16 28.999
5	28 22.138	16 28.450
6	28 22.399	16 28.546
7	28 22.761	16 28.631
8	28 22.814	16 28.702
9	28 22.883	16 28.795
10	28 22.982	16 28.891
11	28 23.095	16 28.958
12	28 23.180	16 29.090
13	28 23.249	16 29.137
14	28 23.339	16 29.227
15	28 23.316	16 29.042
16	28 23.418	16 29.000
17	28 23.461	16 28.999
18	28 23.480	16 29.024
19	28 23.873	16 28.914
20	28 23.932	16 29.048
21	28 23.979	16 29.098
22	28 23.970	16 29.006
23	28 23.808	16 29.312
24	28 23.952	16 29.302
25	28 24.025	16 29.268
26	28 24.122	16 29.047
27	28 24.132	16 29.389
28	28 23.994	16 29.554
29	28 24.110	16 29.526
30	28 24.155	16 29.525
31	28 24.009	16 29.918
32	28 24.016	16 29.965
33	28 23.321	16 30.048

Montaña Teide photographed while on the Arenas Negras route.

The slumbering volcano of **Montaña Teide** dominates the centre of Tenerife. Rising to 3,718 metres, it is the highest point on Spanish territory. At its foot lies **Las Cañadas**, a vast sunken crater with an average altitude of over 2,000 metres, comprised of huge sand-like plains interrupted by petrified lava flows and mountains in an array of colours from black, sand, grey, gold; there are even rocks in green and blue (**Los Azuelos**), easily seen when driving through the National Park on the south section of the main road.

The first impression on entering the area is of a dramatic, other-worldly place, geologically unique but barren. However, the Teide National park and its environs are home to a surprising number and variety of plants, some endemic. Visit in spring to see the tall, dark red exclamation marks of the red tajinaste (*Echium wildpretii*), amid a sea of white retama (*Spartocytisus supranubius*) set off by the cushion-like yellow of *Adenocarpus viscosus* similar to a dwarf yellow broom. Much rarer, and found almost exclusively on **Montana Blanca** and **Pico del Teide** is the Teide violet (*Viola cheiranthifolia*). As we drop down to the south and west from **Las Cañadas**, forests of *Pinus Canariensis* dominate, cistus, lotus and asphodels thriving in the dappled shade. As for fauna; there are plenty of wild rabbits and lizards, and some beautiful butterflies, and you might see the Hoopoe (*Upapa epops*) with its distinctive black and white wings, the Great Grey Shrike (*lanius excubitor*), the Buzzard (*Buteo buteo*) or the Kestrel (*falco tinnunculus*).

The climate at such an altitude is the most extreme on the island. **Montaña Teide** and the other peaks are often snow-covered during winter, and the ground may well crunch icily beneath your feet if you tackle some of our high altitude walks between November and March. By mid-June the days are hot, and there is very little shade for walkers, and the dryness of the air soon draws any sweat from the body, making it essential to replace fluid regularly even though you may not be aware of thirst. Our 'Paisaje Lunar' and 'Lunar Orbit

2' routes, south of **Las Cañadas**, are still excitingly high altitude, but are just within the pine forest zone, offering some shade for hot weather walking.

The clarity of the air makes for wonderful views, and you will usually be able to see some of the other islands while following these walks. However, the air's thinness makes walking harder work than at lower levels, and there is a risk of altitude sickness if you ascend too quickly - take time to acclimatise before tackling our more strenuous routes at this altitude. We would advise you to try our 'Montaña Majúa - Toffee Mountain' route with climbs and descents of about two hundred metres as an introduction to this high altitude region.

Part of the Lunar Landscape is visible among Canarian pines.

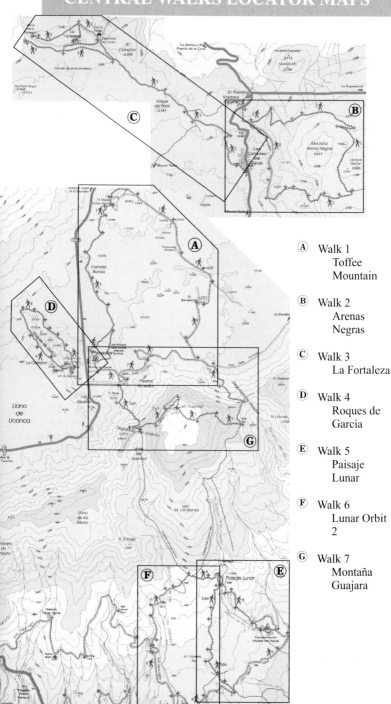

Ⓐ Walk 1
Toffee
Mountain

Ⓑ Walk 2
Arenas
Negras

Ⓒ Walk 3
La Fortaleza

Ⓓ Walk 4
Roques de
García

Ⓔ Walk 5
Paisaje
Lunar

Ⓕ Walk 6
Lunar Orbit
2

Ⓖ Walk 7
Montaña
Guajara

C1. MONTAÑA MAJÚA - TOFFEE MOUNTAIN

Las Cañadas is a big crater with the emphasis on Big. Just drive from **Boca Tauce** to **El Portillo** to see how big this region is. It is just as big on foot as when you are in the car but being in direct touch with this amazing landscape means that the visual illusions are greater. In **Las Cañadas** everywhere looks closer than it is; in fact much closer, as your eyes foreshorten the large distances. Look at **Mount Teide** - it seems as if you could just reach out and touch it!

Toffee Mountain, or **Montaña Majúa**, is our introduction to walking in these high altitudes (2,000+ metres) and if our description tends towards describing the scenery in confectionery terms then blame it on the thin air.

3/4 — 3 hours — 13.5 km — 200m / 200m — 2*

* Catering at **Parador** café.

Park your car at the **Parador**, or jump off the **Parador** buses (Titsa), and wander across to our start point alongside the cafe terrace. We always recommend that you take a ten to twenty minute break when arriving at this altitude to let your body acclimatise before starting walking. The old official start of this route used to be behind the **Parador**, and the old 'diamond' walking signs are still in place but have been sanded back to the aluminium, so we follow the new 'official' route; see map for original route.

From the café, we walk past the hotel entrance and set off down the access road. Keeping an eye to our right we spot the start of 'sendero 19' (**Wp.1, 3M**) signed at the start of a narrow walking trail. We are heading east (**E**) towards a 'caramac' coloured lava flow, passing two more 'sendero' signs (**Wps.2 & 3**) nailed to rocks after which our trail starts to become indistinct in the broken ground. Small stone cairns keep us on route to come along to more 'sendero' signs (**Wp.4, 11M & Wp.5**) before meeting the original path coming in from the right (**Wp.6, 13M**) as we come up to the 'caramac' lava wall. Now the original and new routes have come together we follow the narrow trail as it skirts the wall of lava (**N**). More S19s (**Wps.7, 8 & 9**) are followed by twin S19s (**Wp.10, 20M**), confirming our route as we leave the first lava wall behind to cross a plain towards another lava flow. Coming below the lava (S19, **Wp.11**), more toffee than caramac this time, we skirt this new lava flow. It is an easy stroll to come between two large rocks (S19, **Wp.12**) before passing a possible path off to our left (**Wp.13**) and then strolling along to an interestingly veined rock on the right of our path (**Wp.14, 30M**), looking as if it has been laminated from different rocks.

Our sandy path, rather like dune walking, moves out from the lava wall for a while before curving back guided by small cairns towards an obsidian finger of rock (**Wp.15**) followed by S19s (**Wps.16 & 17**). More small cairns guide us as the 'crunchy bar' coloured mound of **Montana Majúa** comes into view and a small valley is on our right. We come into a broken landscape (S19 at

Wp.18, 46M, S19 **Wp.19**) of spiky rock outcrops before starting to walk up a water runoff (**Wp.20**), cairns again confirming our route in the direction of the cable-car station. The small valley ends (**Wp.21**) as we come up to a 'Peligro Colmenas' (**Wp.22, 56M**), (danger - bees), sign and then pass a second sign on our right (**Wp.23**). On our right is a small ridge which runs up to **Montaña Majúa** and we go right (**Wp.24**) to climb across the open 'crunchy bar' ground onto the line of the ridge to find a *sendero* (**Wp.25**) heading up towards the rounded peak. We make no excuses for our slow progress up the steep trail, the thin atmosphere requiring a number of breaks before we reach the trig point (**Wp.26, 71M** and 2,353 metres altitude on our GPS).

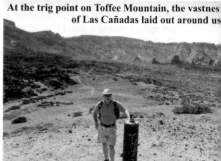

At the trig point on Toffee Mountain, the vastness of Las Cañadas laid out around us

From the trig point of 'toffee mountain' (**0M**) we go gently uphill (**NE**) to pass piles of lava stones as we cross the peak to come onto a faint walking trail which drops down towards the **Pista Sanatorio**. Before descending, we can see the roofs of the **Sanatorio** away to the south-east of us, our next destination. We come down the trail, passing a path off to our right (**Wp.27, 6M**) as we come onto the *pista* (S16) to walk past a junction where another *pista* goes off to our right. **Pista Sanatorio** has a good walking surface, allowing us to make relaxed progress while taking in the subtle colourations of the rock formations in this region. Three strange metal covers (**Wp.28**) are passed on our left as we bowl along the dirt road to pass a path off to our right (**Wp.29, 17M**) just before our route curves right to run gently downhill. We come down to a strange sight at a junction (S16, **Wp.30, 22M**), where a bunker appears to have been concealed in a rock mound. If you take a couple of minutes to walk up to the locked door you will see that the 'bunker' contains the large pipes of the system used to capture the snow-melt off **Mount Teide**; those metal covers are also part of this water system.

Leaving the 'bunker' behind we stroll along passing an S16 sign (**Wp.31**) before passing a *pista* off to our left (S16s and **Wp. 32**). The **Sanatorio** roofs come into view on our right (**Wp.33**) just before our *pista* curves between large rocks (**Wp.34**) to come to the **Sanatorio** entrance (**Wp.35, 45M**); just the place for a pleasant break after that power walking.

From the **Sanatorio** (**0M**) we continue on the *pista*, passing a path and *pista* off to our right (**Wp.36**), with the **Las Cañadas** cliff wall rising ahead of us. An easy stroll brings us past a *pista* to the right (**Wp.37**) to negotiate a metal barrier across the main *pista* (**Wp.38**) - hurdle over if tall enough, or duck under - before we come down to the 'Siete Canadas' *pista* (**Wp.39, 15M**) alongside the cliff wall.

If you are looking at your GPS in this location, you might notice it producing funny readings. The vertical escarpment is cutting off satellite reception to the south of us giving unreliable readings; not that you will need any navigation devices for the next stage, which is along the **Siete Canadas** *pista* heading west.

Now we join the walking motorway of **Las Cañadas** for an easy stroll as the *pista* climbs and twists along below **Montaña Guajara**. We continue ascending until we come along to a left curve with panoramic views down over the **Parador** (**Wp.40, 32M**). Now it is downhill as the *pista* curves left and then right, passing a path (**Wp.41**), before coming to the vehicle barrier (**Wp.42, 45M**) just before the tarmac starts. In a relaxed stroll down the tarmac it is all too easy to miss the small path off to the right (**Wp.43**) that leads to the **Parador**. Leaving the tarmac, we follow the faint trail across the lava, to come onto a little-used *pista* (**Wp.44**) which we follow westwards (**W**) until we come to a path off to our right (**Wp.45, 54M**). On the path we come up to the **Las Cañadas** notice board (**Wp.46**) on the south of the **Parador**, and in a few more metres we are back at our starting point on the café terrace, three hours from the beginning of our walk.

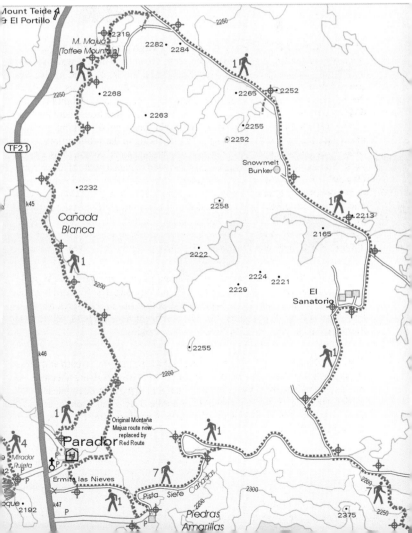

C2. BLACK SAND SURPRISE - ARENAS NEGRAS

For exciting views you just cannot beat altitude, so for our first high mountain walk we have chosen the little-known **Arenas Negras** route from the **Visitors' Centre** at **El Portillo**. We climb 300-plus metres, but it happens so gently that you hardly notice; the views expand and expand, and as if that isn't enough, the ground opens at our feet into a great chasm. Skitter down the side of a black sand cliff, and we have a terrific introduction to the excitements of **Las Cañadas**.

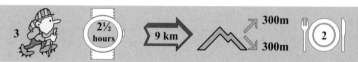

We start out from the extensive parking area at the **Visitors' Centre** close to **El Portillo**. Across the road (**Wp.1, 0M**) we go past the barrier on the **Siete Cañadas** dirt *pista* to cross a shallow valley before coming up to a junction of *pistas* (**Wp.25, 5M**) where we go left (*sendero* 2) on the minor *pista*. We have a gentle ascent (**ENE**) in amongst the tundra, a very soft landscape compared to much of **Las Cañadas**, on what was once a dirt road though no one has driven this route for years, so gradually nature is reclaiming the route.

Our *pista* swings right (**Wp.2, 13M**) to head south (**S**) before swinging back **ENE** and gradually narrowing to walking trail width (**Wp.3, 26M**) hemmed in by bushes of Teide broom (Spartocytisus supranubius). Below us is the scenic TF-24 road across the high *cumbre* to **La Laguna**, as views ahead open up over the **Orotava Valley** and **Puerto de la Cruz**, the **Los Realejos** *cumbre* looking particularly impressive from our elevated position (**Wp.4**). Our path is climbing very gently, almost contouring around **Montaña Arenas Negras** and bringing the top of the **Izana** observatory into view (**Wp.5**) just before pushing through bushes of Teide Broom (**Wp.6**) which try to overwhelm the path.

After the easy contouring, our path starts a steady ascent (**SE**) to bring us up to a hairpin bend (**Wp.7, 48M**) where confused walkers have created short false paths, giving the impression of a trail junction. Keeping right, we continue ascending through more Teide Broom (**Wp.8**) to a second hairpin bend (**Wp.9, 56M**) by large rocks and a small cliff. More of the **Izana** observatory comes into view as we traverse the lower slopes of **Montaña Arenas Negras**, gradually swinging south (**S**) as we climb. Our route is curving as we ascend between **Arenas Negras** and **Cerrillar** mountains, the ascent gradually easing so that we miss the high point of our route by the magnificent panorama of **Mount Teide** that comes into view.

Now we are back to easy strolling as our trail widens allowing us to take in the panoramas as we progress. We gradually curve **SE** to come to a junction (**Wp.10, 80M**) where the path ahead, with a line of rocks across it, heads towards the *cumbre* and a *sendero* marker (2) directs us right (**W**) on a faint trail. There are small cairns and a *sendero* marker (**Wp.11**) guiding us into a gully which opens into a great chasm at our feet, as more *sendero* markers (**Wps. 12, 13, 14 & 15**) guide us left along the southern side of the canyon to bring the **Las Cañadas del Teide** restaurants into view (**Wp.16, 88M**). If the canyon was a surprise, we immediately come to another as our path takes us onto a black *picon* mountain, our route coming back to the canyon's edge before sweeping left across the steep black slope in a skittering descent to large rocks. Below the rocks, the path is steeper as we zigzag down the black slopes as slowly as practical to keep a sure footing, before the path runs off the slopes down a small gully to a *sendero* marker (**Wp.17, 105M**). Our route steepens for another skittery descent on black *picon* before coming down to the floor of **Las Cañadas**, the black mountain and giant canyon dominating the landscape behind us.

On the valley floor it is easy walking, but the path is very faint as we head east (**E**) along the left side of a valley, *sendero* markers (**Wps.18 & 19**) keeping us on track until our route runs out to meet the **Siete Cañadas** *pista* (**Wp.20, 118M**). Turning right (**N**) we stroll along the *pista*, which is quite pleasant but nothing like as exciting as our earlier route, passing *sendero* signs (**Wp.21,123M**) and a short stiff ascent (**Wp.22, 125M**) before reverting to easy strolling. An easy stroll takes us past *sendero* markers (**Wp.23**) and a vehicle barrier (**Wp.24**) before meeting our outward route at the *pista* junction (**Wp.25, 138M**) and then up to the main road (**143M**). You can savour this route a second time by driving up to the most southerly of the **Las Cañadas** restaurants, from whose terrace you have superb views across to that skittering black *picon* mountain descent, and the huge canyon that we nearly stepped into.

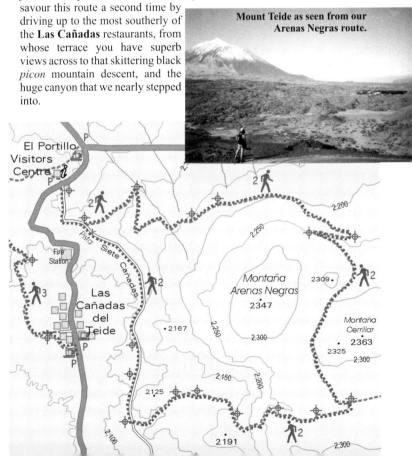

Mount Teide as seen from our Arenas Negras route.

C3. LA FORTALEZA

La Fortaleza's red cliffs are one of Tenerife's classic high altitude walking routes. Views are spectacular from the peak of **La Fortaleza**, from the western end of the **La Fortaleza** massif, and from the **Riscos de La Fortaleza**, all of which are covered in this route. On a map the route looks straight forward, but the broken ground of **Las Cañadas** combined with the 2,000+ metre altitude are very energy sapping.

Our starting point is at the southern end of the **Las Cañadas del Teide** where we park near the **Bar/Rest Bamby (Wp.1, 0M)**. After walking north (**N**) past the bar we turn left onto a dirt road (**Wp.2**) with a *Peatonal* sign. Behind the bar, the dirt road peters out into a path which becomes manicured with a concrete surface (**Wp.3, 3M**) and in a few metres we pass a branch of the path (**Wp.4**) heading back towards the settlement. It is a surreal experience walking on a man-made concrete path, if somewhat lumpy, through the broken land of the **Cañadas** with Teide broom (*Spartocytisus supranubius*) pushing in on our

route.

After fifteen minutes the concrete ends (**Wp.5, 15M**) for us to continue on a traditional dirt path amongst the spewings of rock, meandering through valleys towards the peaks of **La Fortaleza** and **El Cabezón**, seen from the crests of our route. Dropping into a steeper valley, we cross its water course (**Wp.6, 21M**) to climb up past a piece of manicured path (**Wp.7**) to come to a junction with a stone seat (**Wp.8, 25M**), where Sendero 6 is signed left to **Mount Teide**. In another four minutes we pass the path of Sendero 6 (**Wp.9, 29M**) signed right to **El Portillo**, and an alternative start for the **La Fortaleza** route.

Views open up on our right as we climb steadily through the broken land to pass a Sendero 1 marker (**Wp.10, 38M**) near the edge of the pine forest before swinging westwards. On past a weather station on our right, our route comes through a 'rock gateway' with a Sendero 1 sign (**Wp.11, 43M**), to head north-west for us to come to the top of a slope overlooking the gravel plain below **La Fortaleza** (**Wp.12, 48M**). At the bottom of the rough path we come onto the plain (**Wp.13**) to head towards the *degollada*. The gravel plain becomes a steep sand beach, making the climb up towards the pass doubly difficult until the sand gives out (**Wp.14**). We finish the ascent on a conventional dirt and rock path, passing a path off to our left (**Wp.15, 65M**), to come up to the small *ermita* and **Cruz de Fregel** recreation area set on the *degollada*. **Cruz de Fregel** has seen better days, most of the seats having been taken by trophy hunters leaving just one table under a *choza* roof.

From the *choza* (**0m**) we take a dirt road (**NW**) through the pines which gently climbs past a small memorial shrine (**Wp.16**) before finishing (**Wp.17, 6M**) in open ground north of the **Fortaleza** peak. Clear paths go straight ahead and left, which we take to steadily ascend (**S**) to the peak (**Wp.18, 14M**) and the superb views.

Back at the dirt road (**25M**) we take the second path (**WSW**) which meanders across the massif, passing an interesting rock formation (**Wp.19, 35M**) to come above the cliffs. The path continues past a small peak (**Wp.21**) before running out into an eroded gully (**Wp.20, 40M**). It is a possibility for the foolish and adventurous to scramble down the gully, then going left to meet our later route at **Wp.24**, but this is not for us. Best views are back at the small peak (**Wp.21**) before retracing our route back to the *choza* on the *degollada* (**61M**).

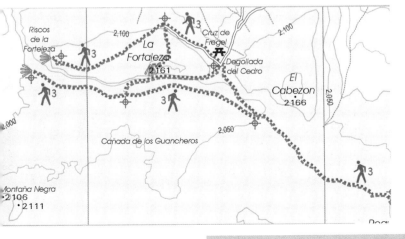

Our second leaving of the *degollada* (**0M**) is on the main trail (**SW**), passing our inward route (**Wp.15**), and swinging down to a vehicle barrier (**Wp.22**) which we step around. The route narrows to a small path with Teide broom pushing in on our route as we stroll along beneath the impressive cliffs of **La Fortaleza**.

This once used to be a dirt road but now is hardly a walking route in places as nature and erosion reclaims the land; secateurs useful. The path demands careful footwork before we come down to the edge of the plain where cairns mark the route out to a junction of paths (**Wp.23, 12M**). Turning west, we follow the trail out to the **Riscos de la Fortaleza** (**Wp.24, 22M**) for the impressive views out over the pine forest to the **Teno** mountains and the north-west coast of Tenerife.

Now it is time to head back to base, retracing our steps back to the edge of the grit plain (**Wp.23**) and taking the general path across this strange phenomenon back to our entry point (**Wp.13**). A stiff climb up the eroded trail takes us back into the broken land of the **Cañadas**. Again, this region of valleys, descents and ascents, is tougher than it looks on the maps as we retrace our steps. Passing the Sendero 6 junctions (**Wps. 9 & 8**) we are glad not to be tackling **Teide** on foot in this thin atmosphere, as we slog through this difficult landscape to arrive back at **Las Cañadas del Teide** and its reassuringly expensive restaurants, **107 minutes** from our second departure from the *degollada*.

The views from La Fortaleza more than justify the climb.

C4. ROQUES DE GARCÍA

Walking routes don't have to be excessively long or strenuous to be spectacular. **Roques de García** is a Tenerife classic, while being accessible and within most peoples easy compass. Spectacular geology gives an interesting viewpoint on the **Las Cañadas** region in a compact tour.

If there is a problem, it is that this route is so accessible you may find yourselves walking with crowds of other walkers. Walk the route in the direction we take, as the reverse direction involves a descent from the **Mirador de la Ruleta**, where boot erosion has made for a slippery, potentially hazardous, steep descent; much easier to climb than descend.

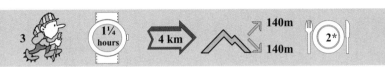

3   1¼ hours   4 km   140m   140m   2*

*Catering at **Parador Café**

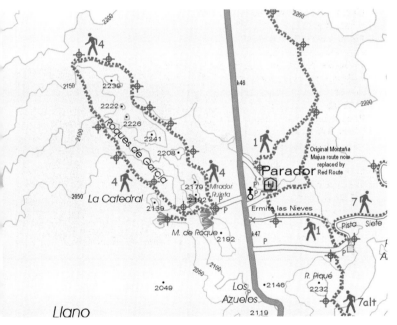

Start early to avoid the crowds, before 10.00am, by parking at the **Mirador de la Ruleta**. From the *mirador* roundabout, viewing paths lead up to the left and right - not part of our route - to give spectacular views down over the **Llano de Ucanca** plain and lava fields. We start out (**Wp.1, 0M**) from the north of the roundabout by following the well-trodden path between the roped off *naturaleza* areas for a pleasant stroll to come along below the impressive, and much photographed, **God's Finger** (**Wp.2**) on our left, and huge clumps of rock on our right which look like building foundations. Our path curves left (**Wp.3**), with an option to go left to a viewpoint over the **Ucanca** plain, becoming very rocky as we pass another ridge on our left to come under cliff walls before another viewing point on our left (**Wp.4**). The rocky underfoot gives way to grey sand as we come along (**NW**) to a pass between a lava field on our right and the impressive rock formations on our left (**Wp.5, 8M**).

A short climb (**Wp.6**) brings us up under the rocks for us to come alongside an area of dark grey 'hippo-backed' lava field on our right (**Wp.7**) before curving left around rock pinnacles to face a large wind-sculpted rock formation (**Wp.8, 17M**); the wind erosion having resulted in 'cartoon heads' of rock on its southern face. We pass a 'Sendero 3' marker (**Wp.9**) and come onto a lava field (**Wp.10**) before coming under the mass of rock for our path to run down its northern side.

Roques de García seen from the Ucanca plain.

Cairns both sides of the path (**Wp.11, 21M**) mark the start of our descent down towards the plain, the rock and scree path making for a slow footstep-picking descent on this section of our route. As we descend, a remarkable 'tree root' system of knotted lava is viewed on our left where it has solidified in the midst of tumbling down between the rock pinnacles (**Wp.12**).

Finally, the scree-covered path descent ends at the start of another hippo-backed lava field (**Wp.13**) which makes for easier progress. Past an 'S3' sign (**Wp.14**) small cairns give guidance across the lava sheet for us to overlook the **Ucanca** plain (**Wp.15**) and pass some classic examples of the Teide wallflower (Erysimum scoparium) (**Wp.16**) before moving across to the east of the lava field (**Wp.17**) to come under buttress-like rock projections, the self-shattering buttresses soaring surreally skywards above us, before we come down to the end of the hippo-backed lava onto a plain (**Wp.18, 45M**).

Now we are on an easy stroll along the grey sand path towards the 'Cathedral', a Gaudi-inspired volcanic creation rising over one hundred metres out of the plain, passing an 'S3' marker (**Wp.19, 50M**) as we come under the great rock. Keeping left we past east of the Cathedral (**Wp.20**) and our path starts a gentle ascent to pass a 'S3' marker (**Wp.21**), and now our path climbs with a bit more urgency. This is a long slogging ascent so pace yourself. Also there are several routes, first up to the saddle and then up to **Mirador de la Ruleta**. We keep with the most climbed route, passing a boulder and cairn (**Wp.22**) before coming up alongside the saddle on our right (**Wp.23, 57M**). Here we take a dirt path (**S**) to the saddle (**Wp.24**) and then on to the *mirador* (**Wp.25**) by a 'mosaic' rock outcrop overlooking the **Ucanca** plain.

Coming back from the *mirador*, we take a higher dirt path back onto the main climb. Now the route splits frequently, we take the steepest uphill route at each option but these grit covered slopes would make a tricky descent. Voices come down to us from above, not a holy experience but crowds of WI tourists released from their coaches line the **Mirador de la Ruleta** above us. Climbing the most energetic section of our route under their watchful eye is rather unnerving and it is a disappointment not to be cheered as we spring across the parapet onto the *mirador* (**Wp.26, 75M**).

C5. PAISAJE LUNAR - A TENERIFE CLASSIC

Paisaje Lunar's unique 'moonscape' geology is one of Tenerife's classic routes which should be on all walkers 'must do' list. The basic route is straightforward, 45 minutes each way. Our route takes an eastern return route via **Campamento Madre del Agua** which takes in a more varied landscape; 120 minutes walking. You also have the option to walk in from the TF-21 junction just above km.66; 6.5kms and 90 minutes each way. For mountain bikers, four wheel drivers wanting a challenging route, and for masochistic walkers wanting a full day in the heights above **Vilaflor**, we include a brief description of the **Agua Agria** *pista forestal* which takes in unusual rock formations and the spectacularly sited 'dead tree' *mirador*.

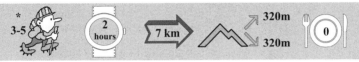

*Basic circular walk, 3 walker, from TF-21 and return, 4 walker, TF-21 to **Paisaje Lunar** and **Pista Agua Agria**, 5 walker.

Pista Madre Agua to Start of Main Walk

Our start point is above **Vilaflor** on the TF-21 just past the km.66 marker where we turn off the main road at the hairpin bend onto a broad *pista forestal* (**Wp.1**). People worried about cruelty to hire cars should park at the side of the *pista* to continue on foot. The *pista* is well stabilised but rough in places, and setting your odometer to zero, we set off along the dirt road, passing a path off to the left (**Wp.2**) and a chained private *pista* to the right (**Wp.3**) before passing a ruined cottage on our left at 2.4km (**Wp.4**).

We pass the barred *pista* to **Galería El Pino** at 3.2km (**Wp.5**) after which we go downhill to cross the water course of **Barranco de las Mesas** and climb the eastern valley wall to come up to pass a ruined cottage on our left (**Wps.6&7**) at 4.4km and a 'Naturaleza' sign. Now we are back to easy strolling, or driving, to pass a forest track crossing the *pista*, 4.7km (**Wp.8**) just before coming to a junction at 4.8km (**Wp.9**).

'Agua Agria' is signed up to the left as we continue front right on the main *pista* signed 'Barranco Rio (sin salida)'. We cross the municipal boundary 'TM Granadilla' at 5.1km (**Wp.10**) to come up to a *pista* off to our left, 5.3km (**Wp.11**) signed 'Agua Agria' and the route of our 'masochist' option. A forest trail is passed at 5.6km (**Wp.12**) just before a more major junction, 5.8km (**Wp.13**), where a cobbled donkey trail goes left and a barred *pista* runs off to our right. Past another chained *pista* off to the right, 6.1km (**Wp.14**), we come to the start of car parking along the side of the pista (**Wp.15**) and the path junction, 6.5km (**Wp.16**), for the 'official' start of the **Paisaje Lunar** walking route.

Main Walk

At the start of the path (**Wp.16, 0M**) a sign informs us that **Paisaje Lunar** is

45 minutes, **Valle de Ucanca** 3 hours, **Degollada de Guajara** 3 hours 45 minutes, as we set off along the stone-lined trail through the pines to pass a second sign (**Wp.17**) before coming to a cross-roads of paths (**Wp.18, 7M**). **Paisaje Lunar** is signed to the right, and we keep left in a couple of metres to follow the main path steadily uphill through the young pines. This is an easy woodland path meandering through the forest before climbing over a small hump (**Wp.19**) and then running out into a lava field (**Wp.20, 13M**).

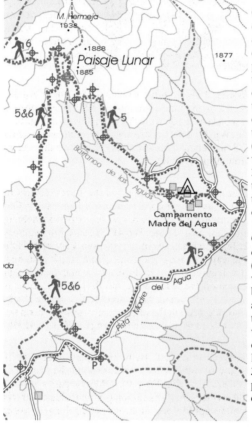

Our route comes up over the lava (**Wps.21 & 22**) and we are climbing through pines again (**Wp.23**) to come up to catch our first glimpses of the white pumice rock of **Paisaje Lunar** through the pines (**Wp.24, 25M**). A white arrow (**Wp.25, 28M**) confirms our trail as we climb up to the highest point of our route (**Wp.26, 1,866 metres on our GPS**) before we start dropping into a valley (**Wp.27**) to cross the water runoff (**Wp.28**) before coming up past a large Canarian pine to a *mirador* viewpoint overlooking the lunar landscape (**Wp.29, 36M**); one of the best photo opportunities on the route.

The white and beige pumice rocks look very close, but we still have a little way to go as our trail runs along the western wall of a steep valley, cistus bushes adding to the mature pines and *retama*, to cross the water runoff (**Wp.30, 43M**). We come up past another large pine to a path junction (**Wp.31**); left up the black *picon* slope is TS8 to **Montaña Arenas**, another path goes straight on, and TS7 is arrowed down to the right. Going right, we come carefully down to cross a watercourse (**Wp.32**) to the edge of the lunar rockscape; most impressive (**47M**).

After taking a break under a large Canarian pine, we continue down the narrow path (**0M**), carefully picking our way down to a watercourse and over to a path junction (**Wp.33**); the left hand path goes up through the lunar rockscape on a higher route to the junction at **Wp.31**. Turning right, we pass

another section of the lunar rockscape (**Wp.34**) before coming onto a woodland path running along the eastern side of this floriferous valley, cushion-like yellow lotus plants lining our route as if deliberately planted there.

Our route swings left (**Wp.35, 10M**) to bring us onto a bare ridge (**Wp.36**) studded with golden needled young pines. We cross a steel pipe to cross a water runoff and on to a second bare ridge where we head down the ridge line, a white arrow on a rock (**Wp.37, 18M**) confirming our route as we cross another steel pipe (**Wp.38**) and come amongst pines to climb up the eastern ridge to another white arrow (**Wp.39, 22M**).

We follow the path down, crossing a steel pipe, as the sturdy chalets of **Campamento del Madre Agua** come into view across a large valley. Our path runs down the spur requiring careful footwork, water erosion not helping the route as we swing left below a large pine (**Wp.41**) to come down to cross the water runoff (**Wp.42, 34M**) and then up onto a *pista* (**Wp.43**) with **Paisaje Lunar** signed back up the way we have come down. From here it is an easy stroll down the dirt road as it curves round to the campsite entrance, though our preferred route is to step off the road onto a trail (**Wp.44**) which leads down to a bare ridge studded with young pines and the first of the sturdy chalets (**Wp.45**). Then it down through the encampment, past the main tap (**Wp.46**) and 'Gualivao' sign on a tree, to meet the *pista* again (**Wp.47, 41M**).

Now the route finding is easy as we stroll down the broad *pista* to a signed T-junction (**Wp.48, 45M**) to turn right. After a short descent the *pista* runs through pines to cross a 'black sand' river (**Wp.49, 49M**) and pass a walking trail off to our left (**Wp.50**) as the *pista* starts climbing. Our apologies for this section, as we face a relentless uphill slope all the way along the *pista* to our starting point (**Wp.16, 68M**).

Pista Agua Agria
Mountain bikers, drivers of tough four wheel drives, and masochistic walkers can enjoy this long *pista* through the mountains above **Vilaflor**. Do not attempt this route in a normal car, or in bad weather. See map for the route which we consider one of the best off road drives (Landrover) in Tenerife but sections can get washed away and unprotected vertiginous drops require full concentration.

From the junction on **Pista Madre Agua** (**Wp.11**) we swing up onto the narrow *pista* to come up to a cute bridge over a ravine (**Wp.51**) before climbing up to a T-junction (**Wp.52**) where we go right; going left will take you back down to the **Pista Madre Agua** at **Wp.9**. Now it is up through the trees (**Wp.53**) and passing a *pista* off to our left (**Wp.54**) plus a crude forest trail off right (**Wp.55**). Now we come to the most difficult section as the *pista* swings along the side of a very steep valley (unprotected vertiginous drops) to run through a region of unusually coloured rocks (**Wp.56**). Sections of the *pista* which have been washed away in previous rains have been crudely rebuilt requiring some skill to negotiate. Coming back amongst the forest, we pass a strangely located threshing circle (**Wp.57**) and eventually climb up the very rough *pista* to **Fire Pine Mirador** (**Wp.58**) where we can take a break accompanied by one of the south's most awesome of views.

After the *mirador*, there is more rough *pista* for us to reach **Galeria Agua Agria** (sour water) from where it is rough going, particularly on the descent down onto the TF-21 just above the km.24 marker. If you have walked this route so far then you have an easy 2km stroll down the TF-21, passing the entrance to **Fuente Alta**'s 'El Pinalito' water factory, to where you parked your car at the entrance to **Pista Madre Agua**.

C6. LUNAR ORBIT 2

Paisaje Lunar is one of Tenerife's most popular high altitude walking routes. For our second visit to the impressive lunar rockscape, we present a western woodland circuit through previously un-surveyed territory. Hire car drivers afeared for their vehicles can reduce the distance driven on the **Madre del Agua** *pista* by parking just after the 'T.M: Granadilla' sign and before the second **Agua Agria** *pista* junction (**Wp.41**).

Masochistic mountain walkers determined to ascend to **Degollada de Ucanca** or **Degollada de Guajara** - only for the extremely fit - should note the junctions at waypoints 19 & 20, which pinpoint the two trails in this previously unmapped region.

3   2½ hours   9.5 km   370m / 370m   0

Our official starting point is reached by driving 6.5 kilometres along the *pista* **Madre del Agua** to the signboard for the **Paisaje Lunar** route (**Wp.1, 0M**). Following the same outward route as for 'Lunar Orbit 1', we pass a second signboard (**Wp.2**) and at a path junction (**Wp.3, 8M**) we go right and left, following the 'Paisaje Lunar' signboard. Our trail takes us steadily up through the woods and onto lava (**Wp.4**), and then a mixture of lava and pine woods (**Wps. 5, 6, 7, 8, & 9**) up to a *mirador* viewpoint overlooking the **Paisaje Lunar** rockscape (**Wp. 10, 40M**). Following our path alongside the steep *barranco* we cross its watercourse and come up to the junction of paths (**Wp.11, 44M**) below a black *picon* slope.

From the junction (**0M**), we trudge straight up the black *picon* (**TS8 & NW**) to a stone marked with a green dot to go left off the black sand (**Wp.12, 3M**) and into the trees (**Wp.13**) where a steep black sand path goes right up alongside the *barranco*. That short example of an energy sapping, black sand, ascent should warn you off old walking guides which use such routes in this region. There are proper rock and dirt ascents to **Degollada Guajara** and **Degollada Ucanca** reached from later in our route. We stay on the woodland path which contours around above the *barranco*.

Here, it is easy to miss our route off to the right (uphill, and **Wp.14**) as the main path leads straight on before petering out amongst the rocks. A steep climb brings us up onto the ridge line where our path swings up the ridge past a white arrow to the western side of the ridge to cross a *barranco* watercourse (**Wp.15, 21M**). Over the watercourse, and we are climbing steeply up another ridge (**Wp.16**) before the gradient moderates and our path, heading west, changes to a *picon* base (**Wp.17**) to come to an unusual 'binocular' sign leaning against a tree. The view over the forest to the ocean is impressive, but hardly justifies a unique sign. Note that the official signs have not been very securely mounted and have been blown down during winter storms, hence the 'leaning against a tree' situation.

Just past the 'binocular' sign, we come to a junction (**Wp.18, 31M**) where, along the path to the right, there is a blown down sign showing 'Paisaje Lunar

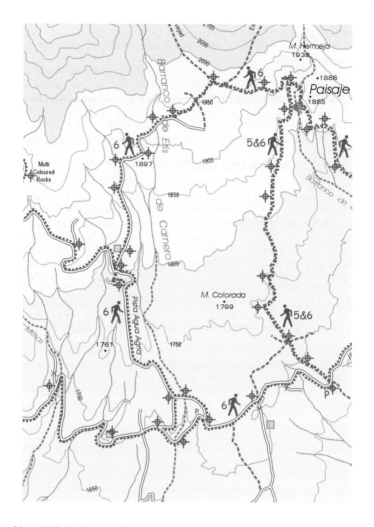

20m, Valle de Ucanca 1hr 15m and Degollada de Guajara 1hr 30m'; for a strenuous ascent to the **Degollada de Guajara**, take the path to the right (**NE**). We continue on the main path, gently downhill now, to pass a 'Valle de Ucanca, Paisaje Lunar' signboard (**Wp.19**) just before the path junction (**Wp.20**) where the **Valle de Ucanca** path goes right (**NW**), and come along to an old water canal (**Wp.21**) with a sign to 'Pista Forestal Madre del Agua 1hr'.

Now our path is fainter (**SW**) as it runs gently downhill through the pines to cross an old forest trail (**Wp.22, 34M**) and pass a small cairn (**Wp.23**) and head towards a survey marker post (**Wp.24**), our trail now on a *picon* base. We come out of the pines into a lava rock landscape for our path to run down a small defile (**Wp.25**) before running out to join a little used *pista forestal* (**Wp.26, 40M**).

Turning right, we follow the rock road down to cross the polished smooth watercourse of the **Barranco de Eris de Carnero** (**Wp.27**, no sign - see map) and continue downhill across a ridge (**Wp.28**), after which the *pista* is very water eroded as it runs down past a rock 'cannonball' (**Wp.29**) on our left. Our *pista* gets smoother and just as it levels out, swings right (**Wp.30**) to drop into a valley with eroded pumice cliffs on our left facing young green pines on our right. We cross a small watercourse and continue downhill, the *pista* becoming more eroded until we cross another water course (**Wp.31**). Now it is easy strolling through the pine woods to pass a dilapidated cottage on our right (**Wp.32**) just before we drop down quite steeply, on a very eroded section, to meet the **Pista Agua Agria** (**Wp.33, 65M**).

We can either cross over **Pista Agua Agria** to continue on a path (see map) or stroll down the *pista*, both routes coming together at **waypoint 34**. Again it is easy strolling with no chance of getting lost (water culverts at **Wps.35, 36** & **37** plus a pair of iron posts at **Wp.38** merely acting as markers for our route) until we come to a junction (**Wp.39, 86M**). Keeping left on the main *pista* we drop down to cross a cute bridge spanning the **Barranco de Eris de Carnero** (**Wp.40**), much more impressive at this lower crossing, before dropping down to meet the **Pista Madre del Agua** (**Wp.41, 90M**); our alternative start and finish point. Turning left, we stroll along the *pista* passing a trail on our right (**Wp.42**), followed by a donkey trail left and *pista* right (**Wp.43**), before arriving back at our start point (**103 minutes** from **Paisaje Lunar**).

C7. MIGHTY GUAJARA

Montaña Guajara dominates the sharp escarpment which encloses the southern wall of **Las Cañadas**. From the **Parador** this mountain, with the sheer cliffs ringing its summit, looks indomitable. In truth it is a straight forward, if very strenuous, ascent by our chosen route. We include the alternative descent/ascent as a warning, not just because it is difficult, complicated and potentially dangerous (it is all of these things), but because it is, surprisingly, the most walked route.

When we start the two ascent sections, you will notice how thin the air is. Not so noticeable is how much you sweat, so take three ½ litre bottles of water each and drink them en route. **Guajara**'s plateau summit can be cold and windy, so take a jacket no matter how good the weather looks. Do not be misled by the walk description appearing in some guide books, this is a tough route described by authors who have been there!

5   4½ hours*   10 km   720m / 720m   0

*but add time for breaks

On arrival in **Las Cañadas** we start by taking a break in the **Parador** café (if open) to acclimatise to the altitude, and then drive to the **Los Roques** road to park near the barrier. Bus riders should alight at the **Parador** and follow our 'Toffee Mountain' route in reverse, to our start point at the vehicle barrier at the start of the **Siete Cañadas** *pista* (**Wp.1, 0M**).

We start out with an easy stroll along the **Siete Cañadas** *pista*, curving around the honey-yellow **Piedras Amarillas** rocks in a gentle climb. As the *pista* comes up to take a climbing loop we step off onto a faint trail (**Wp.2, 10M**) for a steady zigzag climb up its shale surface, easier to ascend than descend, to rejoin the *pista* (**Wp.3, 14M**). Now we are back to easy strolling to loop into a valley with a huge tilted rock looming over us, while **Montaña Guajara** is high above us to the south. We stroll down past the **Sanatorio** dirt road (**Wp.4, 27M**) and now we need to keep a sharp eye for a path on our right (**Wp.5, 32M**), marked by a pair of cairns.

Leaving the **Siete Cañadas** crowds behind, we follow the path (**SE**) in a steady climb with the yellow-lichened cliffs of **Guajara** above us on our right. It is a clear path but the thin air soon takes effect as we climb in lazy zigzags (**Wps. 6** to **13** are path markers) pushing our way through Teide broom (*Spartocytisus supranubius*), also known locally as 'Retama del Teide', which threatens to take over our route in places. At lower altitudes this would be an easy ascent, but at over 2,200 metres altitude it seems like a major climb as we toil relentlessly upwards. Our reward comes as we crest the ridge onto the **Degollada de Guajara** (**Wp.14, 68M**) which is well equipped with magnificent views over **Las Cañadas** (**N**) and down the **Barranco del Río** (**S**), plus some comfortable rocks to sit on while taking a break. On the *degollada* a path comes in from our left, a very strenuous ridge route from **El Portillo**, and another path off to the right while our route is straight over the

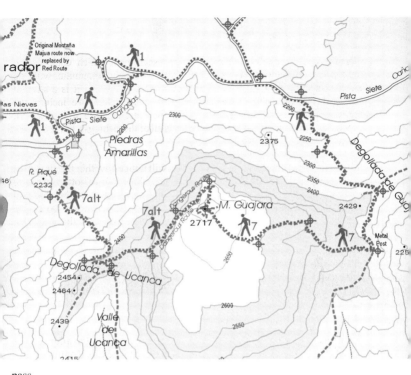

pass.

Suitably refreshed, we set off from the **Degollada de Guajara (0M)** on the main path (**SW**), descending past white rocks as the path curves around the huge bowl at the head of **Barranco del Río**. A short descent (**Wp.15**) brings us under white pumice cliffs before our path starts climbing up through a tumble of rocks (**Wp.16**) for us to come to a junction (**Wp.17, 8M**) marked by a blue and white metal post. Ahead we can see the path running down a black *picon* ridge towards **Paisaje Lunar**, as we turn right (**W**) to start the long ascent to the summit of **Montaña Guajara**.

Small cairns assist wayfinding along the faint path as it takes to a small eroded gully (**Wps.18** to **23** act as direction finders) for a breathless ascent in the ever thinner air. A steady relentless ascent, with plenty of breaks, brings us to the end of the gullies and onto a slippery white and mauve *picon* path lined with small cairns (**Wp.24, 32M**) to pass a path off to our right (**Wp.25, 38M**). It is onwards and upwards on the path (**Wps. 26 & 27**) until we come to overlook a sharp gully (**Wp.28, 53M**).

Here the 'official' path takes a precipitous drop into the gully so to avoid this 'potential accident' we go right up a small *picon* ridge to come onto stony ground where we curve left to rejoin the path (**Wp.29, 57M**). Path is perhaps too grand a word as it frequently disappears amongst the stones and Teide broom. We keep heading upwards (**NW**) towards the ridge guided by cairns and waypoints (**Wps. 30, 31 & 32**) to come onto the plateau summit (**Wp.33, 77M**).

Magnificent views from the summit of Guajara.

After that thin air ascent it is worthwhile taking a break by strolling around the plateau taking in the different views. At the centre of the plateau is a large rock enclosure which even contains a stone table and stone seats! While on the summit, you might look around for the Trig point shown on military maps and pointedly mentioned in another walking guide book; we've been all over this summit and cannot locate any Trig point!

OK, enjoyed the views, and now it is time to descend. Our strong recommendation is that you return by the same route we ascended, avoiding that precipitous gully. The paths are straightforward, with generally good grip, and this time walk down the **Siete Cañadas** *pista* rather than the short cut path. About **120 minutes** will see you back at the vehicle barrier in good shape.

Alternative descent (but <u>not</u> recommended)
The route we describe here has everything you do not want in a descent; scrambling above vertiginous drops, difficult way finding (eased by PNF tracks and waypoints), slippery paths (where there are paths), crossing rock falls, intrusive Teide broom, slippery and slidey shale covered paths. This route is difficult, complicated, dangerous and uncomfortable; we only include it because it is the most popular descent from **Montaña Guajara**, and perhaps to show that we really do do exciting descents! In anything less than perfect weather, or if you feel at all unsure about this route, go back and descend by our upward path.

14.38, 17 February 2003, weather; clear blue skies with light breeze. We leave the **NE** corner of the rock shelter (**Wp.34, 0M**) taking the clear path (**N**) downhill to awesome views down over **Las Cañadas** and to our car. We pick our way down through a jumble of large cuboid rocks (which end at **Wp.35**) to a junction (**Wp.36**) where a short path runs out to a survey marker above vertiginous cliffs. Back at the junction we go west, carefully looking for the cairns which mark the route, to come to a rockfall of large boulders requiring careful scrambling (**Wps.37, 38 & 39**) progress before we come onto a normal walking path, crossing a small scree field before our path runs below the cliffs and bulk of **Montaña Guajara**. We say normal path, but this is a slippery pumice *picon* descent, before coming to what we call a normal path (**Wp.40, 26M**). Next is a large rockfall (**Wp.41, 33M**) which we climb through; by now we are getting an appreciation of this route! A 'nougat' style rock on our right (**Wp.42**) cheers us as we come into the sunshine as the cliffs have changed from brown to slate grey as we come under the cliffs again making steady and careful progress. We move out from the cliff wall (**Wp.43, 40M**) to follow the path steeply down (**Wp.44**) through rock detritus (**Wp.45**) to negotiate a fall of giant scree followed by a slippery pumice *picon* slope to bring us to a rock ridge (**Wp.46, 57M**). It seems a bit churlish to add that most of the scrambling and slippery sections take place above massive vertiginous drops down to **Las Cañadas**!

At the rock ridge, we look out onto a very different tumbled landscape of mature Teide broom thriving on a steep rock-dotted hillside that runs down to the path junctions on **Degollada de Ucanca**. It is certainly less dangerous than the earlier section, here it is difficult to fall further than a couple of metres, but easier; no. In the tumbled rocks beneath the broom its twist left, twist right, scramble down, and then repeat it all again and again and again. Various paths, and cairns, have been pushed through the unforgiving vegetation. We follow what seems to be the main path (**Wps. 47, 48, 49 & 50**) before arriving at a huge knob of rock (**Wp.51, 73M**). A bit more twisting and shoving (**Wp.52**) and we come out into the open (**Wp.53**) to stroll (!) down onto the *degollada* (**Wp.54**) and over to the path junction (**Wp.55, 79M**) where the path up the **Valle de Ucanca** joins us. Take a break, drink another ½ litre of water, and mentally prepare for the final descent.

From the *degollada* (**0M**), a clear path drops down and goes left (**W**) to a path junction (**Wp.56**). Our main path turns sharp right to descend on a tricky rock shale surface below a north facing cliff. Carefully picking our footsteps, we move out from the cliffs onto the 'Thousand Zig-Zags' descent, passing a nice rock tower (**Wp.57**) on our left before coming down (**Wp.58** path marker) to a split in the trail (**Wp.59**) with both routes cairned, before they come back together again (**Wp.60**). There are more twists and turns before our route straightens out (**Wp.61**) to bring us onto a manicured yellow rock path (**Wp.62**); oh the luxury! At a large rock (**Wp.63**) the luxury ends and we are back on a rough trail which brings us along to cross the water runoff beside the tarmac road (**Wp.64, 40M**) and a short stroll on this beautiful tarmac brings us back to our car (**45M**).

Teleféricos (cablecars) are a wonderful way of climbing mountains, allowing even the least energetic to enjoy the same views as fit mountain walkers. You can walk up **Montaña Teide**, but it is one long hard slog with the rating for effort way off our scale. When you do get up there make sure you haven't forgotten your 'Pico' pass from Icona's office in Santa Cruz, or you won't be allowed up to the peak.

If you must walk on **Mount Teide**, why not cablecar up and walk down, a long descent and tough on the knees. For a good description of both the ascent and descent of **Teide**, look at Mike Reid's website:-

www.fell-walker.co.uk/andalus.htm

Montaña Blanca is a popular ascent - only 400 metres compared to Teide's 1,400 metres. You can park by the start of the jeep track (limited parking) or a little further along the TF-21 by the K40 marker. Just keep slogging up the jeep track, following the crowds, and remember to go left onto **Montaña Blanca** when the masochists go right to continue their ascent on **Teide**. When you do get to the top, you do have terrific views but it still feels a bit of a let down having the vast bulk of Mount Teide looming over you. Better by far, in our opinion, is the ascent of **Montaña Guajara** and the views from its plateau summit.

Every walking guide book for Tenerife, except this one, gives a detailed walk description of the 'Siete Cañadas' *pista* which crosses the crater from the **Visitors' Centre** near **El Portillo** to emerge on the TF-21 just below the **Parador** and the **Roques de Garcia**. At fourteen kilometres the *pista* is long, but the last thing you need is a detailed guide as once you are on the *pista* you simply walk along it until you get to the other end; is has to be the least complicated walking route in Tenerife! Amazingly groups of walkers are 'guided' along this most simple of routes.

This is Tenerife's 'walking motorway', and we do not feel that pages of description will enhance the experience. At weekends every José and his family plus dog is wandering the 'Siete Cañadas' across **Las Cañadas**. All you have to do is find the start at either end and then follow the crowds.

'Siete Cañadas' is easy with straightforward navigation, but the route has one problem. When you reach the other end you are fourteen kilometres from where you started. Few people fancy repeating this walk in reverse to get back to their car (total 28 kilometres), so here is our 'Siete Cañadas' tip. Find another car driver who wants to walk this route. Drive up to **Las Cañadas** in convoy and then at the **Visitors' Centre**, or on the **Siete Cañadas** tarmac side road, drop one car driver with that car's keys. Drive to the other end of **Siete Cañadas**, park and lock the car. When you meet in the middle of the **Siete Cañadas** *pista* swop car keys and then when you get to the end, after fourteen kilometres of ambling along, your car will be waiting for you.

*from Visitors' Centre
**catering at Parador café.

See the notes on GPS use and waypoints in the introduction on page 11.

C1. TOFFEE MOUNTAIN

Wp	N	W
1	28 13.446	16 37.566
2	28 13.477	16 37.503
3	28 13.496	16 37.493
4	28 13.585	16 37.389
5	28 13.612	16 37.346
6	28 13.626	16 37.322
7	28 13.649	16 37.317
8	28 13.700	16 37.295
9	28 13.749	16 37.324
10	28 13.809	16 37.358
11	28 13.888	16 37.377
12	28 13.993	16 37.497
13	28 14.043	16 37.527
14	28 14.116	16 37.543
15	28 14.353	16 37.581
16	28 14.361	16 37.599
17	28 14.480	16 37.518
18	28 14.518	16 37.466
19	28 14.550	16 37.443
20	28 14.581	16 37.465
21	28 14.653	16 37.461
22	28 14.722	16 37.406
23	28 14.771	16 37.386
24	28 14.799	16 37.382
25	28 14.818	16 37.335
26	28 14.913	16 37.329
27	28 14.956	16 37.137
28	28 14.905	16 37.059
29	28 14.669	16 36.672
30	28 14.377	16 36.593
31	28 14.211	16 36.349
32	28 14.108	16 36.255
33	28 13.937	16 36.278
34	28 13.902	16 36.292
35	28 13.912	16 36.312
36	28 13.923	16 36.375
37	28 13.562	16 36.511
38	28 13.544	16 36.502
39	28 13.388	16 36.407
40	28 13.466	16 37.040
41	28 13.397	16 36.938
42	28 13.200	16 37.169
43	28 13.152	16 37.232
44	28 13.275	16 37.305
45	28 13.276	16 37.477
46	28 13.347	16 37.515

C2. ARENAS NEGRAS

Wp	N	W
1	28 18.143	16 33.875
2	28 18.128	16 33.556
3	28 18.022	16 33.321
4	28 18.076	16 33.229
5	28 18.106	16 32.956
6	28 18.092	16 32.907
7	28 17.957	16 32.654
8	28 17.965	16 32.744
9	28 17.976	16 32.807
10	28 17.359	16 32.675
11	28 17.330	16 32.750
12	28 17.321	16 32.795
13	28 17.306	16 32.806
14	28 17.306	16 32.883
15	28 17.322	16 32.915
16	28 17.329	16 32.973
17	28 17.324	16 33.140
18	28 17.399	16 33.307
19	28 17.389	16 33.398
20	28 17.304	16 33.580
21	28 17.468	16 33.560
22	28 17.569	16 33.546
23	28 17.959	16 33.695
24	28 17.979	16 33.749
25	28 18.013	16 33.789

C3. LA FORTELEZA

Wp	N	W
1	28 17.548	16 33.807
2	28 17.569	16 33.817
3	28 17.602	16 33.892
4	28 17.618	16 33.958
5	28 17.893	16 34.031
6	28 17.984	16 34.252
7	28 18.003	16 34.307
8	28 18.030	16 34.405
9	28 18.110	16 34.484
10	28 18.305	16 34.732
11	28 18.360	16 34.986
12	28 18.524	16 35.176
13	28 18.607	16 35.300
14	28 18.720	16 35.397
15	28 18.782	16 35.428
16	28 18.887	16 35.580
17	28 18.928	16 35.670
18	28 18.804	16 35.676
19	28 18.782	16 36.009
20	28 18.838	16 36.149
21	28 18.811	16 36.112
22	28 18.755	16 35.449
23	28 18.689	16 35.832
24	28 18.767	16 36.207

C4. ROQUES DE GARCÍA

Wp	N	W
1	28 13.306	16 37.747
2	28 13.403	16 37.769
3	28 13.448	16 37.818
4	28 13.501	16 37.848
5	28 13.597	16 37.947
6	28 13.642	16 38.030
7	28 13.725	16 38.087
8	28 13.809	16 38.151
9	28 13.808	16 38.178
10	28 13.812	16 38.214
11	28 13.827	16 38.312
12	28 13.788	16 38.315
13	28 13.726	16 38.280
14	28 13.708	16 38.278
15	28 13.669	16 38.262
16	28 13.640	16 38.256
17	28 13.589	16 38.199
18	28 13.489	16 38.118
19	28 13.380	16 37.989
20	28 13.344	16 37.944
21	28 13.321	16 37.923
22	28 13.302	16 37.875
23	28 13.288	16 37.862
24	28 13.269	16 37.864
25	28 13.274	16 37.898
26	28 13.300	16 37.767

C5. PAISAJE LUNAR

Wp	N	W
1	28 09.826	16 37.958
2	28 10.232	16 37.808
3	28 09.937	16 37.633
4	28 10.264	16 37.436
5	28 10.270	16 37.148
6	28 10.064	16 36.903
7	28 10.086	16 36.891
8	28 10.114	16 36.770
9	28 10.137	16 36.704
10	28 10.129	16 36.576

Wp	N	W
11	28 10.152	16 36.508
12	28 10.152	16 36.387
13	28 10.242	16 36.287
14	28 10.291	16 36.166
15	28 10.294	16 36.032
16	28 10.284	16 35.998
17	28 10.352	16 36.085
18	28 10.426	16 36.175
19	28 10.538	16 36.239
20	28 10.657	16 36.238
21	28 10.725	16 36.214
22	28 10.752	16 36.221
23	28 10.762	16 36.226
24	28 10.954	16 36.223
25	28 11.019	16 36.226
26	28 11.062	16 36.211
27	28 11.154	16 36.185
28	28 11.217	16 36.190
29	28 11.244	16 36.151
30	28 11.367	16 36.173
31	28 11.374	16 36.168
32	28 11.374	16 36.148
33	28 11.338	16 36.122
34	28 11.323	16 36.095
35	28 11.218	16 36.067
36	28 11.222	16 36.011
37	28 11.070	16 35.959
38	28 11.039	16 35.942
39	28 11.025	16 35.905
40	28 10.979	16 35.817
41	28 10.922	16 35.794
42	28 10.922	16 35.758
43	28 10.910	16 35.740
44	28 10.902	16 35.747
45	28 10.869	16 35.677
46	28 10.838	16 35.601
47	28 10.854	16 35.537
48	28 10.797	16 35.366
49	28 10.671	16 35.462
50	28 10.650	16 35.479
51	28 10.240	16 36.583
52	28 10.228	16 36.631
53	28 10.257	16 36.665
54	28 10.637	16 36.846
55	28 10.764	16 37.063
56	28 11.034	16 37.269
57	28 10.592	16 37.614
58	28 10.590	16 37.928
59	28 10.935	16 37.984
60	28 10.543	16 38.587

C.6

LUNAR ORBIT 2

Wp	N	W
1	28 10.281	16 35.993
2	28 10.353	16 36.082
3	28 10.425	16 36.169
4	28 10.660	16 36.229
5	28 10.717	16 36.214
6	28 10.759	16 36.223
7	28 10.858	16 36.258
8	28 11.016	16 36.223
9	28 11.227	16 36.189
10	28 11.260	16 36.146
11	28 11.377	16 36.163
12	28 11.385	16 36.185
13	28 11.384	16 36.196
14	28 11.348	16 36.191
15	28 11.335	16 36.265
16	28 11.335	16 36.286
17	28 11.334	16 36.374
18	28 11.341	16 36.424
19	28 11.350	16 36.473
20	28 11.343	16 36.478
21	28 11.330	16 36.495
22	28 11.292	16 36.540
23	28 11.261	16 36.569
24	28 11.253	16 36.588
25	28 11.244	16 36.628
26	28 11.232	16 36.643
27	28 11.198	16 36.707
28	28 11.176	16 36.749
29	28 11.157	16 36.786
30	28 11.107	16 36.762
31	28 10.975	16 36.858
32	28 10.748	16 36.851
33	28 10.672	16 36.894
34	28 10.638	16 36.851
35	28 10.381	16 36.826
36	28 10.367	16 36.739
37	28 10.309	16 36.684
38	28 10.263	16 36.674
39	28 10.233	16 36.639
40	28 10.241	16 36.591
41	28 10.156	16 36.511
42	28 10.147	16 36.394
43	28 10.245	16 36.289

C.7

MONTAÑA GUAJARA

Wp	N	W
1	28 13.189	16 37.172
2	28 13.391	16 36.936
3	28 13.406	16 36.888
4	28 13.378	16 36.409
5	28 13.321	16 36.223
6	28 13.230	16 36.162
7	28 13.195	16 36.127
8	28 13.191	16 36.110
9	28 13.183	16 36.092
10	28 13.167	16 36.086
11	28 13.132	16 36.109
12	28 13.111	16 36.074
13	28 13.061	16 36.014
14	28 12.988	16 35.893
15	28 12.897	16 35.924
16	28 12.839	16 35.951
17	28 12.784	16 35.914
18	28 12.782	16 35.969
19	28 12.790	16 35.993
20	28 12.783	16 36.024
21	28 12.775	16 36.078
22	28 12.790	16 36.118
23	28 12.803	16 36.132
24	28 12.830	16 36.150
25	28 12.877	16 36.188
26	28 12.875	16 36.228
27	28 12.878	16 36.259
28	28 12.821	16 36.399
29	28 12.810	16 36.431
30	28 12.824	16 36.509
31	28 12.859	16 36.538
32	28 12.895	16 36.575
33	28 12.926	16 36.611
34	28 12.934	16 36.608
35	28 12.988	16 36.593
36	28 13.000	16 36.587
37	28 12.997	16 36.611
38	28 12.968	16 36.615
39	28 12.962	16 36.626
40	28 12.935	16 36.647
41	28 12.916	16 36.689
42	28 12.902	16 36.716
43	28 12.850	16 36.771
44	28 12.810	16 36.806
45	28 12.798	16 36.814
46	28 12.777	16 36.843
47	28 12.765	16 36.856
48	28 12.754	16 36.864
49	28 12.757	16 36.876
50	28 12.756	16 36.894
51	28 12.769	16 36.908
52	28 12.768	16 36.930
53	28 12.763	16 36.950
54	28 12.745	16 36.984
55	28 12.729	16 37.040
56	28 12.740	16 37.081
57	28 12.826	16 37.052
58	28 12.908	16 37.130
59	28 12.918	16 37.163
60	28 12.922	16 37.177
61	28 12.951	16 37.215
62	28 12.966	16 37.233
63	28 13.002	16 37.205
64	28 13.149	16 37.234

A snow-capped Mount Teide dominates above western Tenerife's pine-clad slopes.

Tenerife's west coast is an interesting mix of small towns and tiny hamlets, thinly sprinkled along a rugged coastline and inland on dramatically rising foothills and mountains. The region enjoys high sunshine figures, and is rarely troubled by cloudy skies. The massive bulk of **Montaña Teide** offers some protection from the occasional unpleasant *calima* winds from Africa, making the west's climate attractive for walking.

The rugged nature of its mountains, *barrancos*, and plunging cliffs justify our 'wild west' label, the untamed feel pervading up to the boundaries of the settlements which form oases of civilisation planted in the beautiful but sometimes savage landscape. Petrified *malpais* lava fields flow down almost to the outskirts of towns and villages, and are some of the harshest and most unforgiving landscapes on the island - walkers need well-cushioned, tough footwear.

Particularly striking are the strong, contrasting colours of western Tenerife; white villages, black lava fields, rich red-brown garden plots, hazy green terraces, cobalt seas foaming white at the base of grey cliffs - a photographer's delight.

Wild plants cover a wide range of species, from many varieties of tough, drought and wind-resistant euphorbias and *plocama pendula* on the lower, exposed coastal areas, through to the white daisies of *Argyranthemum* frutescens, wild figs and agaves, almonds and olives, to the beginning of the tree-line with Canarian pines and some eucalyptus. The rocky mountain sides support a surprising range of plant life, including some of the island's endemic succulents, clinging to apparently soil-less crevices.

An *aeonium* clings to a rocky outcrop.

There are few wild animals other than rabbits and goats, although bird-watchers will not be disappointed, and there are many species of insects and lizards to look out for. Birds to watch for include the Linnet (*Acanthis cannabina*) Canary (*Serinus canaria*) and Whimbrel (*Numenius phaeopus*).

In common with the rest of the island, this region has undergone changes as tourism has developed into Tenerife's most important industry. Even so, the lack of accessible beaches has restricted such development in the west of the island to the short coastal strip between **Los Gigantes** and south to **Playa de la Arena**, and agriculture remains an important source of income.

Around most towns and villages are farmed areas, as the volcanic soil is rich when irrigated; bananas, citrus fruits, tomatoes, peppers, marrows, potatoes and papayas are a few of the crops raised on *fincas* and in back gardens. When viewed from high ground inland, the larger plantations covered with plastic or fabric can easily be picked out, though the painstakingly terraced slopes higher up are more often left uncultivated now.

Man-made terraces are still clearly visible, even though many on higher ground are no longer cultivated.

Road access has improved by leaps and bounds over the last few decades, and reliable bus services manage to get to most of the towns and villages, including those which were almost inaccessible, such as **Masca**. But even with recent improvements to communications and services, this beautiful side of the island remains 'Tenerife's Wild West'.

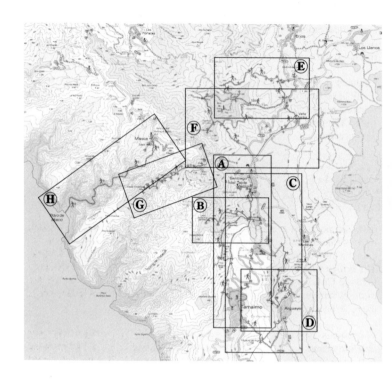

(A) Walk 1   Wild West Tour

(B) Walk 2   An OK Corral

(C) Walk 3   True Grit

(D) Walk 4   Lasso La Hoya

(E) Walk 5   Laurel & Hardy

(F) Walk 6   Saddle Up And Round That Mountain

(G) Walk 7   Picnic At Hanging Rock + Guegue

(H) Walk 8   Survival Of The Fittest

W1. WILD WEST TOUR

Little-used paths (by walkers) take us down the western edge of the valley below **Santiago del Teide** through a mixture of bucolic countryside before coming onto a spectacular ridge for *mirador* views over the 'Wild, Wild West' before descending on an old donkey trail to **Tamaimo**. Exceptional examples of endemic flora pack our route which soon leaves civilisation, though the distant sound of traffic is always with us.

Intended as a relatively leisurely linear walk, you can make it circular using the final section of our 'True Grit' route up to **El Retamar**; then either 'True Grit' across the *malpais* and its alternative finish to **Santiago del Teide**, or from **El Retamar** take the *camino rural* (our choice) up to **El Molledo** to join our outward route.

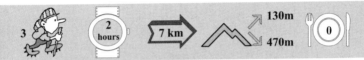

3   2 hours   7 km   130m / 470m   0

Our start point is the centre of **Santiago del Teide** by the **Masca** junction, opposite the church, (**Wp.1, 0M**). Strolling south along the pavement we come to the ornate arch and bridge (**Wp.2, 5M**) for the **Fuente de la Virgen**. The bridge takes us over a water course, and under a second arch we come onto the **Camino de la Virgen de Lourdes**. A dirt trail takes us across the meadow before we start to climb an out-flung spur of **Montaña Ijada**, where the route becomes a stone-laid donkey trail.

The route is 'way marked' by fourteen two metre-high crosses (in very poor condition), each with a plaque depicting a stage of the **Calvario**. Once past the first cross, we have an energetic climb as we ascend, following the signed route after the third cross (**Wp.3**) rather than taking the short cut to the sixth cross. At a spoil heap a dirt path goes straight ahead (**Wp.4**) while we continue ascending on the stone-laid trail. The steady ascent finally brings us to the fourteenth cross where the trail swings right to climb diagonally across the slope to a *mirador* at a hairpin bend overlooking the village. After taking in the views we ascend through the hairpin bend to make a last climbing traverse across the slope, which brings us up the flower-bedecked *ermita* (**Wp.5, 15M**) set in a rose bower.

Suitably breathless, we can admire the *ermita* and the views over **Santiago del Teide**, set off by the dramatic backdrop of the golden lichen-covered cliffs of **Montaña Ijada**. Suitably refreshed in soul we pick our way back down the same route to **Santiago del Teide** (**30M**). Continuing south on the pavement we pass the garage to come to the signed *sendero* 'Santiago - Los Gigantes 7,720m 2.5hrs but provisionally finishing in Tamaimo' (**Wp.6, 32M**) opposite **Bar Jardines del Valle**; the last refreshment opportunity until **Tamaimo**.

We step out along the broad grassy trail (**S**) with the slopes of **Montaña Ijada** away on our right, easy walking through this bucolic landscape of stone-walled fields only occasionally in cultivation. The main road has swung away east as we pass a copse of stately palms on our left and a collapsed terrace wall

(**Wp.7**), and here the gentle nature of the route starts to change as the trail narrows and drops down between high boulder walls on a lumpy stone-laid base, before continuing as a dirt path which runs alongside abandoned fields. The trail becomes increasingly stone-littered as we descend gently towards **El Molledo**, looking over the village as our path runs across a large slab of rock at the end of a spur. The views then open up down to the ocean, the path becoming rough as it descends above cultivated plots to meet the wide stone-laid donkey trail of 'An OK Corral' (**Wp.8, 42M**). Down below us is the second way marking sign for the continuation of the 'official' *sendero*, and an alternative return route for a circular walk, as we turn right to climb up (**W**) over rock to a path junction (**Wp.9, 44M**).

'OK Corral' takes the right fork while we go down to the left.

The rock and dirt trail with occasional stone-laid sections which takes us steadily down the valley wall (**W**), great swathes of coloured rock and vertically grained rock 'fences' running down from the steep slopes above us. A steel water pipe runs alongside our route as we turn round a spur (**Wp.10, 51M**) to see our trail running ahead around the valley wall. It is downhill on the rough path, crossing a boulder-choked gully (**Wp.11**), before undulating along to the corrals (**Wp.12**) and buildings (**Wp.13, 57M**) of the goat farm.

The farm's large flock of goats look cute but have churned up our path beyond the farm, so careful footwork is needed as we climb over a spur and into a pocket in the valley wall, before our route climbs higher above the valley floor to an outcrop of red rock making a natural *mirador* (**Wp.14**). From the outcrop we pass **Fuente Chiñagana** leaking water into two small pools, suitable only for animal consumption. Beyond the *fuente* we continue on the gritty, goat-churned path (**S**), dropping then climbing up to a saddle on the ridge (**Wp.15, 67M**). Once on the ridge before **Roque del Paso** we are treated to an impressive western panorama, including **Roque Blanco** and **Barranco Mancha de los Diaz** - camera essential.

From the saddle, our route drops steeply down the western side of **Roque del Paso** on a boulder-laid trail. Our trail becoming littered by rock flakes which have shattered from the rock face on our left before taking on an alternately flat then up-and-down nature to reach a junction on another saddle (**Wp.16, 77M**), south of the peak. The views in this area are all five-star.

A Diversion
Our onward route goes east (**E**) at this point, though the energetic can take a demanding diversion into the **Barranco Mancha de los Diaz**. Continuing on the southerly trail, we zigzag steeply into the *barranco* on a deteriorating trail down the sheer *barranco* wall, our concentration rewarded as we reach a 'lawned' promontory, suspended beneath the mountain and the *barranco*, surrounded by superb views. It is a picnic spot with few equals. Although the trail continues down **Barranco Seco** to the sea, then climbing 800 metres to **Morro de la Vera**, due to the deteriorating trail, high vertigo risk and sheer endurance required, we recommend only our short diversion to the 'lawn'. We return by the same route to the saddle.

Continuation
From the saddle we take a little-used path (**NE**) which runs below the eroded southern face of **Morro de la Vera**. This path was made for the tunnel workers, there is a water canal runs from **Tamaimo** to **Barranco Mancha de los Diaz**, and the goats keep open much of the western section but our route has suffered from erosion and is becoming overgrown; secateurs very useful. Concentration is necessary on the overgrown loose boulder trail, as we head downhill to a hairpin bend, secateurs useful as we progress along traverses and through hairpin bends. After hairpin Nº9   we come below a large cave, the peak now hidden from view, and after hairpin Nº13 we encounter a large fallen rock, followed by a fallen terrace wall a little further on. Picking our way over the stones, we come back onto the path which winds down the slope to join the route of the 'official' *sendero* (**Wp.17, 89M**).

For a circular route, turn left (**N**) and follow the trail back up to **El Molledo**.

Turning right (**S**) we follow the narrow trail downhill alongside a steel water pipe; the pipe swinging left across the watercourse (**Wp.18**) just before a faint walking trail (**Wp.19**) follows the pipe. Its a steady trudge down the path to pass a large pine (**Wp.20, 100M**) and abandoned terraces above our route (**Wp.21**) before coming down to a junction (**Wp.22, 106M**) where a little used stone-laid trail climbs to our front right. Here we turn left to skitter down a rock laid slope to cross the water course onto slabs of rock. Curving south we continue on the rock slabs until we spot a glass-littered dirt path (**Wp.23**) which takes us up to the first houses of **Tamaimo** (**Wp.24**) and onto a tarmac street. At the end of the tiny street we are at a T-junction; left is steeply uphill and then right to climb up to the top of the town; easier by far is to go right and then work our way through the old town to the main road (**117M**) and refreshments.

W2. AN OK CORRAL

If you are looking for a simple, safe route into the spectacular *barrancos* of the west coast, this walk is for you. With easy bus or car access, well-made trails and stunning views, this route has everything except a refreshment *tipico*.

3 | 100 mins | 5 km | 170m / 170m | 0

Our start point is the main road bus stop and shelter for **El Molledo** village by the 'El Molledo - Los Quemados - Risco Blanco' sign; reached on the 325, 460 and 462 Titsa bus services. Car drivers should turn off the main road at the bus stop and park by the village square and church.

From the bus stop, we follow **Calle La Tagora** to the village square and church (**Wp,1, 0M**). Coming to a cross roads, we continue straight over (**W**) onto **Calle Calzada** and drop steeply downhill until we face house **N°16**.

Here we turn right on a track between white walls and boulder walls to cross a water run-off (**Wp.2**) and come onto a stone-laid donkey trail. The trail climbs up to a junction (**Wp.3**) where the route down to **Tamaimo** is signed left, while we continue to climb steadily, to another junction (**Wp.4**) where the path from **Santiago del Teide** comes down the hillside to join us. Keeping to the main path, we come to a third junction (**Wp.5, 5M**) where a path runs down the wall of the valley (our 'Wild West' route), while our route is the higher path to the right.

We start a steady, continuous climb up around the edge of a bowl in the valley wall, the lower path running parallel but soon far below us. Excellent views (stop to look) compensate for the energetic ascent on a mixture of stone-laid trail and rock slopes in reds and yellows (**Wp.6**). Across the bowl we notice another pair of way marking posts, and the gradient eases as we approach a corner in the bowl. Just past the corner, a Madonna statue and cross occupy a cave (**Wp.7**) just above the path, and our trail continues as a comfortable dirt path which leads us to the way marking posts, which are missing their signboard, and the **Fuente Tenengueria** built in 1936 (**Wp.8, 14M**) with a working water tap.

The path is easy to follow as we leave the posts and *fuente* behind and resume our ascent of the plant-covered slope as the track swings west (**W**), flattens out and then climbs again, our narrow path wriggling up towards the ridge line above us. In this barely accessible, seemingly uncultivateable land, a stiff climb brings us up to two tiny walled terraces (**Wp.9**) set in a small pocket in the valley wall, our route zigzagging steeply past them. In places the route is not clearly defined as it crosses sheets of rock, but a low stone wall keeps us on track, and we reach a purple rock *mirador*, just the place to take a break and enjoy the panoramic views across to **La Hoya**.

Views across Barranco Mancha de los Diaz, to La Gomera (in cloud) in the background.

Notice the natural rock arch in the ridge above us as we set off again, on a gentle ascent up to a precariously balanced large boulder (**Wp.10**). Scuttling beneath the boulder, we descend into a pocket in the valley wall where our trail turns left above a large cleft. Grasses push in on the narrow path as we stroll (**S**) between the ridge and the long drop to the valley floor, the ridge becoming gradually less prominent as it comes down to meet our path (**Wp.11, 31M**). Now new vistas open up across **Barranco Mancha de los Diaz**, and following the line of the ridge we zigzag down onto a saddle - the views are impressive!

From the saddle we go down the knobbly rock sheets, following the line of a low boulder wall to reach a trail which we take down into the head of the *barranco*, a steep, almost staired descent which then levels out to follow a contour line around the bowl in the head of the *barranco*. We curve around towards abandoned terraces, the goat farm hidden from view as we climb up through the terraces towards an overhanging rock outcrop, from where (**Wp.12, 43M**) we enjoy stupendous views along the length of the west. A cairn of white-splashed rocks mark the path's continuation off the outcrop leading us onto a clearly defined trail which heads towards the goat farm with its fences, gates and noisy guard dogs (chained). The couple who run this isolated agricultural enterprise 'commute' from **El Molledo**, carrying the goat feed with them! An old threshing circle (**Wp.13, 47M**) alongside the corral makes an 'OK' *mirador*, but continuing onto the spur which runs down from the corral to **Roque Blanco** reveals dramatic views into **Barranco del Natero**, while if you look inland you will see tourist hire cars lined up on the distant **Masca** road. Although goat tracks abound, we do not recommend attempting to descend the ridge to **Roque Blanco**, as there is no clear track and this landscape is potentially dangerous.

We return by the same route, there being no other safe way.

W3. TRUE GRIT - A WESTERN CLASSIC

Some walks have it all; varied landscapes, spectacular views, masses of endemic flora, great geology and refreshments. This is such a walk, with the added advantage of *tipicos* located just where you need them! Surprisingly, no other walkers appear to know of this route, so you won't be bothered by multi-coloured paint splashes spoiling the natural beauty. Definitely a 'Western Classic'.

Our start (and finish) point is the T-junction in **Tamaimo** where the **Los Gigantes** TF-454 road meets the TF-82 main road coming round the mountains from **Guia de Isora**. Buses from **Playa de las Américas**, **Playa de la Arena** and **Los Gigantes** serve **Tamaimo** or for a less strenuous walk take the 462 bus as far as **Arguayo**, saving an hour of walking and the main 350 metre climb. Car drivers will find plenty of on-street parking around the T-junction in **Tamaimo**.

4   2¾ hours   9 km   430m / 430m   3

We start out (**Wp.1, 0M**) by walking south (**S**) on the **TF-82** road where a gentle uphill stroll brings us to **Calle La Rosa** on our left (**Wp.2, 3M**). Turning left we climb up this steep street, passing **Calle La Ladeira** (**Wp.3**) on the left, to the last house (**Wp.4, Nº13**) at the back of which the tarmac finishes.

We continue on a rough *picon* trail bounded by a rock boulder wall, the bulk of **Montaña del Angel** looming over us on our right, and the peak of **La Hoya** with its antennae away on our left. Old rock walls line the path as we come up a ramp and step over a working water canal (**Wp.5, 7M**), continuing to crunch upwards, the original boulder-laid donkey trail occasionally showing through. Our route swings gently east (**E**), flourishing endemic plant life threatening to take over the route (secateurs useful). Swinging right round a Canarian pine brings us to an impressive *mirador* (**Wp.6**), a good place to get one's breath back.

Our steady ascent continues between pines, the boulder wall on our left splashed with a white paint boundary marker. The gradient begins to moderate and we look down into a valley populated by a showcase of endemic flora below **Montaña del Angel** on our right as we head up into a bowl in the valley wall. The path widens for a short section before shrubs start to occupy the route once again, secateurs useful. Now we face a loose scree, the boulder walls that accompanied us heading off left and right. Ignoring the faint path to the right we follow the left wall (**NE**), a faint trail emerging as we progress. Coming to a hole in the wall, we swing right to continue climbing (**S**) which brings us onto a stone-laid donkey trail which takes us zigzagging upwards, the trail's base disappearing, then reappearing briefly, boulder walls to left and right. Above us, a cave in the slopes of **Montaña del Angel** seems like a portal in a sci-fi movie - or it could be the effects of altitude and exertion! We continue our climb, terrace walls coming into view above us, and **Arguayo** stands out clearly on the ridge behind us. A final *tabaiba* inhabited slope (**Wp.7**) where it might be easier to walk up the left hand stone wall, brings us onto a dirt and rock road (**Wp.8**) where a gentle slope brings us up to the end of a *camino rural* (**Wp.9, 32M**) on top of the ridge alongside the terraces under **Montaña del Angel**.

Before charging off towards **Arguayo** (**N**) we take a gentle stroll on the dirt road (**S**) to where it drops down the slopes towards the road, where a donkey trail begins; a few metres detour down the trail gives us impressive views down to **Playa la Arena**.

After this interlude we stroll along the *camino rural* for a hundred metres to where a donkey trail goes left (**N, Wp.10**). At this point you can take an easier alternative to **Arguayo** by following the *camino rural* up to cross the TF-375 (**Wp.12**) and then turn left up the old main street to **Bar El Cercado**; see map.

Our traditional route is along the donkey trail following the line of a boulder wall towards **Arguayo**, climbing steadily on the trail's mix of *picon*, original stone-laid surface and occasional volcanic blowholes, like rock-rabbit burrows. At a solitary pine our trail turns right and up to a crest facing the village before descending to cross a shallow terraced valley where *tabaiba*, marguerite and broom push in, making those secateurs useful again. Climbing again towards the village is laborious on the fist-sized *picon* rocks, as we pass a trail (**Wp.11**) which runs down towards **Tamaimo** and face a final grit slope up to the TF-375. Carefully crossing the road we go up a dirt track alongside a red house onto the village's main street to the welcome sight of **Bar El Cercado** (**Wp.13, 55M**) where we recover with suitable refreshments.

After R&R (recovery and refreshments) we set off up the steep main street of **Arguayo** (**0M**) to the bus stop and shelter just past **Taller y Museo Alfarero** (**Wp.14**) where we turn left to cross the new road and come onto a steep concrete lane with a staired centre (**Wp.15, 6M**). When the centre stair finishes, above a triangular *embalse* on our left, we go left onto a walking trail which passes between the terraces (**W**); continuing up the concrete lane is our 'Lasso La Hoya' route. Our route becomes a boulder-laid donkey trail climbing up the steep slopes below the peak before the gradient moderates (**Wp.16**). We stroll under sculpted cliffs and then swing north (**Wp.17, 12M**) bringing views across the **Tamaimo** valley and to the knobbly peak of **Roque Blanco**. After an easy stroll the path changes to rock as we begin energetic climb towards a crest in the trail (**Wp.18, 19M**) before descending gently towards a spur which runs down from the main ridge. The spur ends in a massive rock outcrop, suspended precipitously over the long drop to the valley floor. Large boulder sentinels guard

'Large boulder sentinels guard each side of the path as it crosses the spur,' twenty four minutes into the walk.

each side of the path as it crosses the spur (**Wp.19, 24M**).

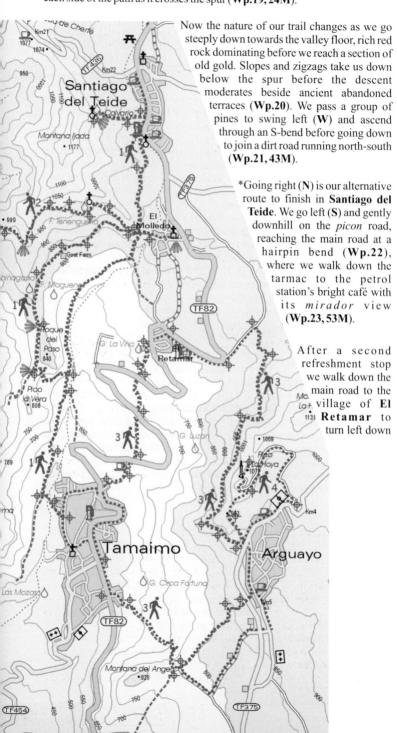

Now the nature of our trail changes as we go steeply down towards the valley floor, rich red rock dominating before we reach a section of old gold. Slopes and zigzags take us down below the spur before the descent moderates beside ancient abandoned terraces (**Wp.20**). We pass a group of pines to swing left (**W**) and ascend through an S-bend before going down to join a dirt road running north-south (**Wp.21, 43M**).

*Going right (**N**) is our alternative route to finish in **Santiago del Teide**. We go left (**S**) and gently downhill on the *picon* road, reaching the main road at a hairpin bend (**Wp.22**), where we walk down the tarmac to the petrol station's bright café with its *mirador* view (**Wp.23, 53M**).

After a second refreshment stop we walk down the main road to the village of **El Retamar** to turn left down a narrow street (**Wp.24**) which cuts off the main road's hairpin bend, and on meeting the main road (**Wp.25**) again we cross straight over to go down a dirt lane past **Casa de Tejas** (**Wp.26**), with its noisy dogs, beyond which the lane peters out and we go left onto a narrow walking trail. Although overgrown with grass, this boulder-laid donkey trail is in good condition, bringing us down past a horse and chickens enclosure (**Wp.27**) to cross straight over the main road (**Wp.28**) to continue steeply down towards **Tamaimo**.

Endemic flora flourish as we swing left at a Canarian pine, giving views up to our earlier route below the peak of **La Hoya**, before crossing the main road again (**Wp.29**), then going left past a small rock outcrop and to a concrete water pipe which accompanies our descent between stone walls with its gurgling. A gentle uphill, and the pipe disappears underground before reappearing as we stroll down to the main road (**Wp.30**) with **Restaurant La Finca** a few metres to our right. Again we cross straight over the road to follow the donkey trail down past a roofed reservoir (**Wp.31**) where the path is temporarily lost under rock rubble. In a few metres the trail reappears accompanied by two steel water pipes and we walk down to come onto a short street (**Wp.32, 81M**) which brings us into the northern outskirts of **Tamaimo**. A stroll down the main street provides plenty of opportunities for more refreshments before we reach our start point at the T-junction with the **Los Gigantes** road. Although the walking time for this route is under three hours (**165M**), we expect your total time to be significantly longer if you have taken proper advantage of the refreshment stops!

Alternative Finish - Santiago del Teide
From **Wp.21** we turn right (**NE**) to walk up to a pine where the red dirt road swings off eastwards (**E**) while we take the donkey trail (**NW**) towards **Santiago del Teide**, crunching along through a rocky landscape well populated by wild plants. With the absence of agriculture, the stone walls come as a surprise - not that they are still in good condition, but that they were built at all. Our loose pebbly path meanders gently up to a small walled meadow, and we pass a well-stocked valley of endemic plants before the landscape changes and we enter the *malpais* where only *crassulas* seem to survive amongst the heaps of volcanic slag spewed across this area. Our route descends gently under power cables before climbing a rock-laid slope to a crest where the trail's nature is emphasised by the breeze-block production works north-east of us. Over the crest, we pass a junction and continue (**W**) to come onto a dirt road.

Across the road, we continue north-west (**NW**) on a path which meanders through the lava spewings. We climb a substantial boulder-laid slope to continue on a pebble path and pass under another set of power lines to go gradually uphill. Rock walls return alongside our route at another boulder laid slope, and the **Arguayo** road and **Santiago del Teide** come into view as we cross a pair of water canals (one in use) into a pathless section. Taking the junction of the main roads as our direction, we pick our way between pits and mounds of volcanic slag, aiming for a group of large boulders which bar vehicle access, beyond which we come down onto the remains of a dirt and *picon* road. Going right, we follow the track up onto the **Arguayo** road. In a couple of minutes we are on the main road's promenade-style pavement, for a relaxed stroll into **Santiago del Teide**, twenty-five minutes after leaving the main route.

4. LASSO LA HOYA

If you only had one hour of walking in Tenerife and wanted to capture as much of the island spirit in this hour, then this is the route for you. It's energetic, rural, modern, terrific geology and flora, exceptional views and finishes at a *tipico*; what more could you ask? Come with us and Lasso La Hoya.

3   1 hour   2.5 km   290m / 290m   3

Take the TF-375 **Arguayo/Santiago del Teide** road off the TF-82 main road and follow the **Arguayo** bypass with the town on your right to park near the football ground. **La Hoya**, meaning valley(!), is the sugar-loaf mountain looming above you to the west.

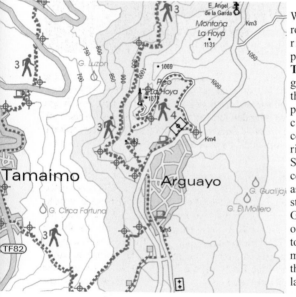

Walking down the road, we keep to the right hand side, passing **Bar/Café Tropic (Wp.14)**, and going on the right of the road when the pavement ends we come to a steep concrete lane on our right **(Wp.1, 3M)**. Steps in the lane's centre help with our ascent and where the stairs finish, our 'True Grit' route goes left on a path, while we toil up the last few metres of concrete to the start of a stone-laid trail.

It is a steep ascent up through the terraces, our trail getting narrower as we go up until we come to a small well on the right of our trail **(Wp.2, 9M)** after which the route seems to go right onto a terrace. Look carefully and we see that the trail continues left, and then right, to climb up a walled channel to a junction of small water canals **(Wp.3)**. A few more metres and we come up onto the *cumbre* **(Wp.4)** - now that's what we call a view; but don't go too near the edge of the sheer cliffs!

Well, if you think that's a view, then follow us **NNE** along the *cumbre* on the left of a stone wall and water pipes to pass a small pylon to come to a water-change point **(Wp.5, 18M)**. From here you could go straight up in a scrambling ascent to the **La Hoya** access road, or follow us right alongside a steel water pipe. Ducking through the pines we keep left to come onto the access road (**Wp.6, 20M**) where it changes from dirt to concrete.

Breathtaking views from La Hoya, even on a day when clouds gather in the valley below.

Turning up the road, we climb up to a hairpin bend above the water-change point (**Wp.7**) to face one big-mother of a gradient. Helpful steps are built into the centre of the very, very steep concrete lane making our slogging ascent a little easier. After a few stops to recover the gradient eases for us to come up to the end of the concrete lane between two transmitter towers (**Wp.8, 27M**).

Now we can have a relaxed stroll up past the second transmitter to the approximate peak of **La Hoya** (**Wp.9**) - don't go too near the edge as there is a 1,000 foot sheer drop, but the views are eye-wateringly impressive. Although the top of **La Hoya** is almost solid rock, you do get some excellent examples of endemic plants. Plant aficionados should look out for examples of the endemic *Lavandula canariensis* (lavender) and the less common small pink asphodel, *Asphodelus tenuifolius*.

There is only one way down unless you have brought your para-glider, so it is back down the road, those concrete stairs proving a boon on the descent on the big-mother. After the end of the concrete (**Wp.6**) you would expect the road to go downhill - well, it's uphill again until we cross the crest (**Wp.10**) and now we have a relaxed downhill stroll, as far as the rough surface allows. We are curving around a lush bowl, surprisingly not in cultivation, with a rough downhill section bringing us onto more concrete (**Wp.11**) before our route runs along to the corner of the football ground (**Wp.12**) and down onto the TF-375 (**Wp.13**). Now it only needs us to throw any excess gear in the car boot and head into **Bar/Cafe Tropic** (**Wp.14** and **23 minutes** from the summit) for some refreshment.

5. LAUREL & HARDY

For once, we move away from the dramatic mountains of the west coast and into a gentler landscape of hills and valleys, though there is still plenty of uphill walking as we experience a surprising range of landscapes within two hours. Laurel forests used to cover vast areas of southern Europe and the Canary Islands, but few pockets of these once-mighty woods remain. The middle section of this route passes through the eerie green stillness of one of these surviving pockets, and the entire route follows dirt roads, paths, *pistas forestal* and tarmac - not a rock climb in sight, resulting in a faster walking pace. With its unique flora, some surreal landscapes and incredible views, this is a route you should not miss.

3   2 hours   6.5 km   300m / 300m   4

We start at the cheerful **Bar/Restaurant Fleytas** on the TF-82 by the **Los Llanos** junction, arriving here by bus or by car. Car drivers should park in the **Fleytas** car park and avail themselves of the cheery service and refreshments after that twisty drive. Leaving the bar (**Wp.1, 0M**), we cross over the road to its southern side and go right to follow the road as it curves through a rock cutting. Just as we come to views down into a bucolic valley, we leave the tarmac on a dirt lane which goes down to our left (**Wp.2**).

We drop down the lane (**W**) between bushes of yellow broom with occasional glimpses into the disused quarrying area on our right. Passing a 'pencil' earth peak, we come down to a bend with views over the lakes and former quarrying area. The lane turns sharp left (**S**) for us to drop down through zigzags on an easy walking surface, though possibly too water eroded for vehicles until we come to a junction (**Wp.3, 7M**). We go right and then left (**Wp.4**) to come to a T-junction (**Wp.5**) where our return route joins us from the left and we take the dirt road going right.

In a few metres we come to another junction (**Wp.6, 10M**) marked by a yellow dot where we go left (**W**) to come up to another junction (**Wp.7**). We go right (**N**) and then stay on the main lane as it swings left (**W**) alongside a dirt wall. Passing a green lane off to our right (**Wp.8**) and then fields occupy former stone pits as we start to climb quite steeply. We stop for a moment (**15M**) to look back at our route before continuing our ascent, the lane climbing steadily up the valley side, once quarried, white broom now established amongst the yellow. Our upward toil continues, the lane now cutting up through tree-heather covered slopes in a long, steep curve towards the south (**S**). Our *pista* now turns

Steeper than it looks in this photo - about fifteen minutes into Laurel & Hardy.

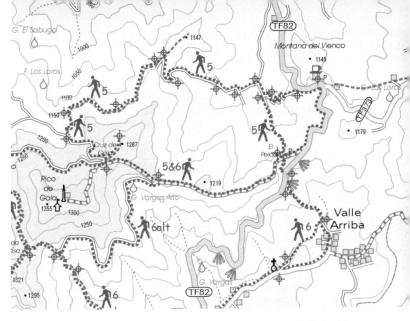

left (**SE**), the gradient moderating before a hairpin bend (**Wp.9, 23M**) with an unused *pista* ahead as we pass a chain vehicle barrier to continue toiling upward, swinging right (**N**) below a slope of Canarian pines.

On the final gradient the tree heather gives way on our right, allowing superb views across the valley and to **Mount Teide** which dominates the distant panorama. A final slog brings us onto the top of the ridge (**Wp.10, 30M**), where a trail leads north off our *pista forestal* along the ridge. For a short diversion we can climb the trail to a copse of pines and on as far as a rough rectangular marker post, from where we enjoy views over **Erjos**. This trail continuing down towards the village, while we return to the *pista*.

On the ridge (**Wp.10**) we follow the *pista forestal* (**SW**) up a gentle gradient to large rocks, where the main lane finishes (**Wp.11**). A rough fire break trail runs up the ridge ahead, as we go right along a narrow path between rocks, immediately after which we enter an ancient, primeval laurel forest. An easy, springy walking path winds along, climbing gently between mossy banks in this green, Tolkein-like environment. The trail comes up to follow a contour line, the steep slopes above and below us laurel-filled, the path unwinding beneath the high leaf canopy. We stroll through the eerie silence, twisting and turning with the folds in the steep valley wall, the atmosphere mystical. There are no views except for the trail ahead and the forest, and we must follow the path wherever it takes us.

We enter an area of older trees, some dead, marked by dark green moss-covered boulders both alongside the path and clinging to the slopes above. Then ferns mark a lighter patch in the forest just before we come to a broken tree barring the path (**Wp.12, 38M** note that there is poor GPS coverage on the following section until **Wp.13**). We duck under and come through a rocky section before the path starts to climb, the forest becoming lighter as we climb from the depths to a crest in the path, then running downhill before swinging back (**SW**) as we negotiate another broken tree. Glimpses of tree-covered hillsides appear through the forest canopy as we ascend past fallen trees and a mossy outcrop, the path climbing steeply and tree heather replacing the laurels as we approach a junction in the path (**Wp.13, 44M**).

We take the left hand path, climbing steeply over a crest before turning back into the forest again, seeming even darker now after that glimpse of sunshine. We follow the path into a small valley, the trail becoming boulder-laid as it climbs a narrow trench to a junction. The southern route is barred by a pattern of sticks, as we swing west (**W**) to continue climbing the same narrow defile, the path zigzagging steeply up to a fallen stone marker post at the edge of the forest (**Wp.14, 50M**). Dappled sunlight falls on us as we ascend through tree heathers, passing another marker stone to emerge into the sunshine and onto a *pista forestal* (**Wp.15, 52M**).

We are on the 'wrong', western side of the ridge so we turn left to walk up the *pista* past a stately Canarian pine, and a yellow diamond walking sign pinned to a laurel. The steady uphill becomes steep as we swing up through an S-bend to another yellow diamond on a tree (**Wp.16**). We continue relentlessly up on this good walking surface until we climb through a bend to a gated and locked junction (**Wp.17, 60M**). Above the junction are large signposts for **El Pelado**, **El Saltadero** and **El Cercado** (the road that we have walked up). On a plinth by the junction is a brass plaque for **Cruz de Gala**, and a north pointer. For a short diversion a path leads up **NE** to a heather covered summit (**Wp.18**)

From **Cruz de Gala** we squeeze past, or climb up alongside, the locked gates to come down onto the tarmac *camino rural* (**Wp.19**) which serves the transmitter and forest look-out on the peak of **Mount Gala** to the south-west; a more challenging diversion rewarded with superb views.

Strolling down the tarmac lane we take in the views over **Valle de Arriba** and **Mount Teide**, and notice the interesting *pista* which runs round the hillside in front of us, an alternative finish on our 'Saddle Up & Round that Mountain' route. If anything the panoramas improve as we come down the lane, in direct contrast to the atmosphere of the old forest. Far below us the TF-82 winds up towards the **Puerto Erjos** pass, and we come under an interesting rock outcrop and onto a saddle to get views of our starting point. At the end of the saddle (**Wp.20**) the *pista forestal* runs down the southern slope away from us. Our easy stroll continues down the broad grassy ridge, dropping down through an S-bend to come alongside abandoned terraces, coming onto a small hill before the lane runs downhill again to another small hill.

We come to a plinth (**Wp.21**) on our left signed **El Pelado** with a north pointer, and just beyond the plaque a traffic sign discourages vehicle access up the lane by a small natural parking area. From **El Pelado** we take the donkey trail dropping down (**N**) towards the lakes, water eroded in places, for us to meet our outward route at **Wp.5**, and then it is back up the dirt road back to our start point and refreshments in **Bar/Rest Fleytas** (**Wp.1, 115M**).

An alternative finish is to continue down the tarmac lane onto the TF-82 and then follow the main road (**N**) for a kilometre to the **Los Llanos** junction and the **Bar/Rest Fleytas**, an easy downhill alternative finish, but take care to walk on the left side of the main road to face the oncoming traffic.

W6. SADDLE UP AND ROUND THAT MOUNTAIN

Breathtaking views combine with a floriferous environment to produce one of the most enjoyable routes in western Tenerife. An energetic start is rewarded by superb flora and exceptional views after climbing onto the saddle at **Degollada de la Mesa**. An ascent onto **Pico de la Mesa**, slightly vertiginous towards the top, brings us the most spectacular views in the region, and that is just the first third of our route. Easy walking takes us out to the **Cumbre de Bolico** and then through the forest to meet our 'Laurel & Hardy' route at **Cruz de Gala**. From the *camino rural* you have an option of a short return on the *pista forestal*, or the longer traditional route down to **Valle Arriba** and an easy stroll back to **Santiago del Teide**.

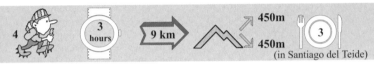

4   3 hours   9 km   450m / 450m   3 (in Santiago del Teide)

Our start is just north of **Santiago del Teide** where we park between the eucalyptus trees just before the **Valle Arriba** road junction (**0M**). We stroll out alongside the main road with the antennae-topped **Pico de Gala** facing **Pico de la Mesa** across the saddle of **Degollada de la Mesa**, our first destination and yes, it is a long way up!

As the main road swings right we step off onto a walking trail signed 'Degollada de la Mesa 1h30m' (**Wp.1, 5M**). Our narrow donkey trail climbs steadily past a stand of large eucalyptus trees and as the vegetation thins out we find a small *barranco* on our right. Endemic flora pushes in on our trail as we keep climbing before swinging right to cross the bubbling stream (**Wp.2, 12M**). On the northern side of the stream, we climb up through tree heather in a series of twists and turns to come onto a rock ledge (**Wp.3, 18M**). It is a relentless ascent so take rests whenever you need them, though relieved by the expanding views and endemic flora.

An all too short flat section is replaced by onwards and upwards with the vegetation thinning out as we ascend to another rock outcrop (**Wp.4, 30M**). Small cairns keep us on the trail as it climbs over sections of bare rock for us to come up onto the end of a *pista forestal* (**Wp.5, 44M**) by a small arrow pointing back down our trail. From

On Degollada de la Mesa - well worth the climb.

the end of the *pista* we take the walking trail heading up towards the saddle, climbing past a rock outcrop (**Wp.6, 53M**) before the final ascent onto the **Degollada de la Mesa (Wp.7, 56M)**. This is a good time to stroll over and take in the western views (**Wp.8**).

Views west and south-east from each side of the saddle are very impressive, but are as nothing compared to the views coming soon. From the saddle (**0M**) a dirt path climbs south-west through the shrubbery, waymarked with green paint. Gradually the path gets steeper and rockier until we turn across the head of a steep *barranco* where trees and plants are bedecked in orange lichen (**Wp.9, 10M**). Our path becomes slightly vertiginous as we negotiate the final section of climb and scramble to achieve the **Pico de la Mesa (Wp.10, 15M)**. From this most orogenical, and rather vertiginous, summit we have the most spectacular views in the west, if you can bear to look at them! Take care on the descent as both the rock and earth can be slippery and surprise the unwary.

Back on the saddle there are a number of paths which can confuse walkers into thinking there is a route up **Pico de Gala**, and their confused walking is making these false paths more prominent. We look for a green arrow on a rock (**0M**) and following its direction we walk along a path which becomes a green tunnel as we pass through tree heather before the path becomes a cobbled donkey trail. Cobbled descents combine with smooth dirt sections to bring us out into the open with beautiful westward views of rugged mountains, deep *barrancos* and high meadows, the broad path now contouring around the head of the **Barranco Madre del Agua** to bring us to a large cairn marking the **El Saltadero** junction of trails (**Wp.11, 12M**).

The main trail continues ahead (**W**) as we turn right onto a smaller path to climb up through the tree heathers onto a *pista forestal* (**Wp.12**) where we go right to another *pista forestal* junction (**Wp.13**). Again we turn right, to walk up the broad *pista* as it steadily climbs between tree heather. After the steady climb the gradient eases, **Mount Teide** is picturesquely framed between the tree heathers at one point and later the red and white antennae on **Pico de Gala** are similarly framed (**Wp.14**) before we come into a region of poor GPS coverage. Finally we come to the peak of the *pista forestal* for an easy stroll down to the **Cruz de Gala** junction (**Wp.15, 27M**) where we meet our 'Laurel & Hardy' route.

Squeezing past the steel gate, we come onto the *camino rural* (**Wp.16**) for an easy downhill stroll. Below us a *pista forestal* contours around the slopes and we meet its beginning (**Wp.17, 35M**) to give us a choice of finishing routes. You can stroll down the *pista forestal* to meet our outward trail at the end of the *pista* and then retrace our outward route down the beautiful valley to the main road, approximately 50 minutes.

Our traditional route is to continue down the *camino rural* until we come to where it is crossed by a donkey trail at **El Pelado** (**Wp.18, 47M**). Going right (**S**), we are on the remains of a donkey trail for a rough descent in a large zigzag to come onto the main road (**Wp.19**) after negotiating a new power pole. Over the road, and in fifty metres, we come to the manicured entrance (**Wp.20**) to the continuation of the donkey trail.

Despite the entrance and a stone wall, this trail has not been maintained and has suffered badly from water erosion making for a slow descent down towards the valley. Some sections of trail are intact (**Wp.21**) but generally the trail gets worse as we descend with the worst saved for last. Just when you thought it couldn't get any worse we come to a narrow cutting that drops us down past vine covered terraces on our right to finally emerge at a power pole (**Wp.22, 65M**) beside a watercourse.

In wet weather we take the dirt road opposite us (**Wp.23**) up to **Valle Arriba** and then follow the road back to our start. In normal conditions we walk along the sandy bed of the water course between stone walls, a stone-laid road joining us from the right (**Wp.24**) shortly before we come onto the **Valle Arriba** road just before the church (**Wp.25, 73M**). From here it is a relaxing stroll through the bucolic landscape back to our start point (**85M**).

7. PICNIC AT HANGING ROCK & GUEGUE

A mixture of donkey trails and paths take us out onto the spectacular ridge which divides **Barranco Seco** from **Barranco de Masca**. Spectacular is an often overused word, but not in this context as our safe but spectacular, and slightly vertiginous, cobbled donkey trail takes us along the very spine of the ridge for the most impressive *mirador* viewpoints. One choice is to picnic at 'Hanging Rock' and return, though energetic hikers will be rewarded for the tough onward route onto the abandoned farmlands of **Guegue**; a true rural idyll protected by fearsome cliffs. Do remember that strolling around the old farmland slopes and descending to view the **Los Gigantes** cliffs has to be paid for on your return ascent. Time and distance is to the top of the **Guegue** sloping plain.

4 | 2½ hours | 10 km | 400m / 400m | 0*

*None on the route, but **Autobar Cherfe** is almost always open, and a man selling fruit is sometimes parked in the *mirador* parking area.

You must get out early if you are going to bag a parking place at the *mirador* just above **Casas de Araza**; even on the pass at **Autobar Cherfe** you might have problems parking later in the day!

If you park on the pass
If you find yourself parking on the pass then here is the alternative to walking down the road (boring and none too safe due to disorientated drivers); walk behind the autobar, taking the lower grit and dirt path (**S**) to drop down to a junction (**3m**) where we take the lower path which turns north (**N**) and continues downhill to a low boulder wall above abandoned terraces.

The path follows the line of the wall (**S**, then **NW**) to the end of the terraces, from where we go down the slope towards **Casas de Araza**. **Barranco del Natero** drops away on our left as we come down onto a natural rock fence overlooking the farm. The faintly marked path runs down off the spur towards the houses, bringing us down to an impressive natural rock fence.

We go left at the end of the wall, where we find a rock descent to bring us under the face of this unusual outcrop. Impressive views open up all around us as we come down to another outcrop, from where we drop down to pick up a path around the low hill in front of the farm and onto a dirt road. The farm's noisy (chained) guard dog is more friendly than its owner, who is probably annoyed by those hikers using out-of-date guides and maps to cut through his farm. We follow the dirt road down into a small valley, and then up a stiff climb to the **Masca** road to join our 'official' route.

If you park at the mirador car park
From the *mirador* car park above **Casas de Aranza** (**Wp.1, 0M**) we walk down the tarmac and step over the chain onto the farm's dirt road (**Wp.2**). A

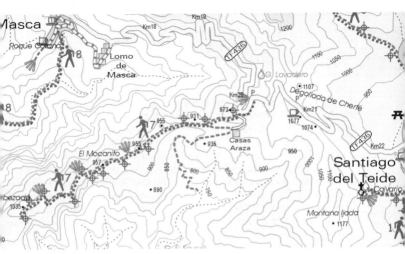

path, signed 'Finca de Guegue' and marked by stone cairns leads us (**W**) through *Plocama pendula* to a little ridge, then dropping down to a junction where we keep to the right hand path.

On this section we overlook the pleasant valley south of us which contains the old route (from when **Casas de Araza** was abandoned). Our route wriggles its way down the slope (**W**) to *mirador* views over **Masca**, then zigzags down towards the huge rock wall which forms a saddle at the end of the mountainous ridge. The path divides, then rejoins just before we come onto the saddle (**Wp.3, 11M**) by a white sign with a double-headed black arrow marking the new route (now lying beneath its mounting post), and a line of boulders across the path which comes down from the farm. A path runs parallel to our route across a valley at the head of **Barranco Seco** on our left (**S**).

From the signboard, we follow the broad trail over the saddle and start to climb up over rock. Our trail takes us past **Barranco Seco** on the left, which soon becomes a steep canyon, while the donkey trail (The Forgotten Trail?) on the far side starts a precipitous zigzag descent into its depths. Our path is littered with rocks as we round a spur to pass through the remains of a pallet gate (**Wp.4**), our onward route heading up a boulder-laid 'drawbridge' (**Wp.5**) towards the ridge ahead. A climb over gold and then red rock (**Wp.6**) brings us onto a boulder-laid donkey trail which runs down onto a saddle, with a *mirador* view down over **Masca**, before climbing another 'drawbridge' to go steadily uphill again surrounded by breathtaking views, then climbing steeply as the well-made trail clings to the sheer walls above **Barranco Seco**, this unprotected sheer drop vertiginous for some walkers.

We come away from the sheer drop to climb a sloping red boulder-laid trail, wider here than on other sections, and the gradient has moderated to a steady uphill, following stone cairns and faded orange way marking as we climb towards the ridge ahead. As we ascend, views open up past **Roque Blanco** down the west coast, the tabletop summit of **Roque del Conde** standing out in the distance on a clear day. Over a rock fence, we come onto sheets of gold, red and brown rock to head up to a line of boulders edging our route. Using stone cairns and occasional orange paint for direction, we continue across sheets of rock on the southern side of the ridge.

As we come onto boulder-laid donkey trail the route swings north-west (**NW**) to a saddle between peaks, blood-red boulders lining the route up to a *mirador* (**Wp.7, 28M**) on blood-red rock looking directly down on **Masca**, **Roque Cataño** seemingly insignificant from this altitude. The route reverts to boulder-laid as it swings towards a craggy peak, our broad, sloping trail drawbridge-like as we climb to it (**Wp.8**). Once off the 'drawbridge', we lose the **Masca** views as we steeply ascend the southern face of the peak, coming out onto more sheets of red rock where stone cairns mark the direction, rock-fence remains dividing the sheets into rectangular sections. Downhill for a short time, then uphill again on a boulder-laid section to a cave (**Wp.9**). Past the cave, we reach the top of the ridge to climb up past an undercut small peak and onto a rock 'table' on the summit. This is our 'Picnic at Hanging Rock' site (**Wp.10, 35M**), surrounded by stunning geology and breathtaking views.

Looking back on our route, the steel gate just visible.

The first section to 'Hanging Rock' is energetic but now the route becomes very energetic as after dropping steeply down under a giant 'five-fingered hand' of rock (**Wp.11** in the heel of the hand) to a steel gravity gate (**Wp.12, 44M**), we face a steep zigzag climb back up onto the ridge (**Wp.13**) for views down to **Masca**. Our path keeps climbing, steep at first but then moderating before running along and swinging right (**Wp.14, 52M**) to pass below a trio of caves (**Wp.15**) before we start another steep zigzag ascent (**Wp.16**).

At the top of this ascent we come to a corner (**Wp.17**) featuring decorative small cairns. **Wp.18** marks our position **60 minutes** from the start. A gentle section leads us to another steep climb that brings us onto the top of the ridge again and spectacular views (**Wp.19, 64M**). Our trail crosses to the west of the ridge running under a great hulk of rock (**Wp.20**), with sheer views on our right, before another steep climb brings us up to the summit of our route beside the peak (**Wp.21**). Now it is gently downhill with the sloping green meadows and terraces of **Guegue** rolling out in front of us (**Wp.22, 75M**).

After all that climbing on hard rock the green meadows and terraces are a welcome relief with colourful chirruping birds flitting amongst the plants, just the place to relax. A path leads over to the remains of a hut, while lower down the sloping plateau you will find the remains of houses. Spectacular views abound from the edges of the plateau, but do remember that there is still plenty of climbing on the return route and exploring down to the old farmsteads will add another 150 metres of ascents to your exertions for the return hike.

8. SURVIVAL OF THE FITTEST

Barranco de Masca is Tenerife's second most popular walk, after **Barranco del Infierno**, but it is not a favourite with us. It's not because the route is extremely strenuous, vertiginous and potentially dangerous in some sections that we dislike it, but it is the only walk on which we have suffered IBS - Irritable Barranco Syndrome! This is a magnificent *barranco*, but you can have too much of a good thing, as you will see on the 'labyrinth' section. You need to be fully fit to undertake the full route to the beach and back; thus the exceptional 6 walker rating for effort. If your fitness is in doubt, then you can walk down the *barranco* and catch the boat from the beach to **Los Gigantes** (Tel: 922 861918 or 860726 for boat times and bookings before planning your walk).

With its incredible landscape, **Masca** is one location where GPS is not suitable for navigation. The high ridges cut off satellites near the horizon, and even with four or five vertical satellites, postional accuracy is poor.

If finishing at the beach, we rate this downhill section only as '4 walkers' difficulty.

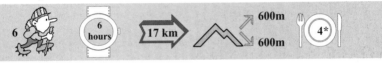

6 | 6 hours | 17 km | 600m / 600m | 4*

*in **Masca**

We start on the road above **Masca** village (**0M**). Drivers should arrive early to secure a parking place near the roundabout, and to allow plenty of time for the walk. One-way walkers and non-drivers should catch the Titsa minibus service from **Santiago del Teide**. From the road above **Masca** we walk down into the village on the broad stone-paved walkway, taking the lower path after the church, signed to 'Chez Arlete'. It's steeply down to rejoin the main paved route and walk out onto the southern promontory. Just before we reach **Bar Blanky**, signed 'BAR' on the outside, there are two wooden posts on the left (**5M**) and a sign which gives the rough time the walk takes (one way only, to the beach) which mark the start of the walking route. You might like to recover from the twisty drive down to **Masca** in the bar while looking down on the first section of the route.

Stone steps lead us down from the wooden posts and onto the 'path', a clutch of steep, slippery, boot-eroded routes down into the *barranco*. Following the line of a rock 'fence', we skitter down to the palm trees where the path divides, where we take the left hand route to continue steeply down. The paths rejoin and the route becomes a little easier as it winds along the northern side of the *barranco*, a section of stone stairs assisting our descent to abandoned terraces. The massive, sheer-sided bulk of **Roque Cataño** looms over us as we come down a stone defile to a 'naturaleza' sign. The path winds down past large rocks onto an outcrop overlooking a wooden bridge. A tricky, vertiginous descent brings us down onto the bridge, where we push through palm fronds to cross it. (**25M**).

Across the bridge, a steep climb followed by a narrow path (**W**) brings us opposite **Roque Cataño**, the *barranco* dropping far below us on the right. Walled terraces, some still cultivated for grapes, line the southern wall of the canyon as we reach a section where the path narrows dramatically, for a vertiginous traverse across a rock slope followed by a scramble, the path then widening to a narrow walking trail as we descend past abandoned terraces, and a stone seat under a palm tree. If you are concerned about the nature of the route this far, take a break in this picturesque spot before heading back to **Masca**.

The path narrows after the terraces and drops down steeply to the *barranco* floor which we cross through a dense bamboo thicket. Up past a large rock, we come onto a proper path which makes for relaxed walking as the *barranco* opens up around us, walled terraces forming a stair on the *barranco* wall as we come to a stone seat, set beneath a shady palm. We now begin a serious descent down rock and boulder slopes to pass under a large rock. Now the canyon narrows, sheer walls almost closing over us as we descend to the watercourse by a large 'cubist' boulder. We continue downhill on the northern side of the watercourse to curve under a huge boulder, a steep descent on boulders polished by hikers' boots. After this narrow defile, the *barranco* opens out as we come below veined cliffs on polished rock sheets towards a low dam wall. Across the watercourse, we continue down to the 'plain' where another *barranco* joins us from the north (**60M**).

Before stepping over the canal at the left of the dam wall and taking the steps down to the *barranco* floor, take a moment to appreciate the beauty of this area, as ahead of us lies the 'labyrinth'. Our path, marked by the brown scuffing of boots, meanders down the floor of the *barranco* as it narrows. Massive chunks of rock dam the defile in this section, and we go under the first of these rock falls, beneath an upended cone of rock (watch out for the large hole alongside the path, big enough to swallow the largest hiker). We scramble down and then across the *barranco* floor to another rock fall. Steeply down the escarpment beside a photogenic waterfall and pool, we then meander across the stream to climb up, following the tortuous route of the defile.

Sheer rock walls fly up hundreds of metres above us as we follow the path, marked by a small cairn of stones, to the unlikely sight of a fence. The *barranco* turns through ninety degrees, and we curve round a large rock to the even more unlikely sight of a green and yellow metal gate, propped open across our path. Again we drop down to the grey pebble *barranco* floor as the path takes us over the watercourse.

Ahead, sunlight streams into the *barranco* where it widens. It's steeply down across another rock fall blocking the *barranco*, crossing the floor again to yet another giant rock fall. This descent is more like caving as we emerge below the fall, to walk down past a stone stair which leads up to the water canal built in the southern wall. Down two more rock falls, we eventually reach a sunlit rock promontory **(1H 40M)**.

It seems as if we are nearing the sea, but this is a false dawn. As the *barranco* widens, another one joins us from the north, creating an airy sunlit area in contrast to the narrow defile we have just come through. We realise that there is still a lot of *barranco* to go before we reach the sea, and are hit by an attack of IBS!

Now you have come to know the nature of this *barranco,* you won't be surprised to find the defile twisting this way and that below immense sheer walls, giant rock falls often with scrambling descents the norm rather than the exception. Often, the path divides and we often seem to pick the most difficult route. Rather than give a step-by step commentary of the journey through this surreal landscape, we urge you to stay on the path. If you come to a seemingly impossible descent, then you have probably taken the wrong route when the path last divided, so backtrack and follow the alternative path. Use the small cairns of stones where they exist, and don't be surprised by steep climbs and descents as these do occur on the correct path, and expect some scrambling descents down giant rock falls.

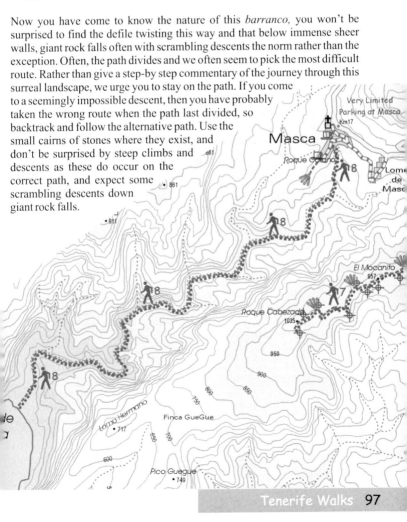

Just as you think that this endless *barranco* will go on for ever, after several attacks of IBS we come to the hopeful sign of abandoned terraces on the southern wall (**2H 35M**). After zigzagging down the terraces and scrambling onto the floor, we climb up the rocks to a turn in the *barranco*. There is blue sky ahead! In our excitement we take the wrong trail along the *barranco* floor, including a 'slide and jump' descent through a massive rock fall. We stagger across the large pebble rocks to reach the beach of **Playa de Masca** (**2H 50M**).

Families of friendly cats share our lunch as we relax on this bay enclosed by sheer cliffs with its single holiday home. Several tourist excursion boats call in, their occupants lurching about on deck or jumping into the sea. If you have pre-booked a boat ride to **Los Gigantes**, take the walkway out to 'pimple island' and join the crowd awaiting a sea borne release.

Our return (**0M**) to **Masca** is tougher than the descent as we face a strenuous 550 metre climb in altitude. After R & R, we set off on the return journey, following a steel water pipe up the south side of the *barranco*, to bring us onto abandoned terraces which bypass our 'slide and jump' descent of our downward route. However, our descent from the terraces is a scramble down a rock wall just past the rock fall, followed by a slippery traverse across rock sheets and back onto our downward route. This path is easily missed when coming down the *barranco*.

Well into the labyrinth, we take a break (**35M**), having already climbed high up the northern wall. We take another break (**60M**), the *barranco* echoing in various languages, 'How much further is it?' from those on the downward route. We reach the stone stair up to the water canal (**1H 30M**) and then avoid the 'slide and drop into a pool' (**1H 45M**) by taking the path up the south side of a huge rock fall. Past the dam, and we sink thankfully onto the stone seat under the palm (**2H**), the abandoned terraces reminding us that we are not too far from the village. We reach another stone seat under a palm (**2H 10M**) at the top of the lawned terraces, and soon after (**2H 20M**) the village of **Masca** comes into sight, high up and far away, as we take care on the vertiginous sections of the path, reaching the wooden bridge (**2H 25M**).

The section after the bridge is the steepest part of our return. We labour upwards, inspired by survival instinct and the sight of **Bar Blanky** high above us. These grit slopes are as potentially treacherous uphill as down, but we emerge between the wooden posts onto the paved walkway having taken almost exactly the same time as on our downward route (**2H 50M**). In one minute more, we totter into **Bar Blanky**, the agua con gas tasting unbelievably good, where we ponder our new attributes as stegophilists.

See the notes on GPS use and waypoints in the introduction on page 11.

1.

WILD WEST TOUR

Wp	N	W
1	28 17.744	16 48.852
2	28 17.577	16 48.807
3	28 17.578	16 48.888
4	28 17.575	16 48.935
5	28 17.593	16 49.011
6	28 17.517	16 48.831
7	28 17.402	16 48.825
8	28 17.149	16 48.856
9	28 17.152	16 48.864
10	28 17.156	16 49.037
11	28 17.136	16 49.064
12	28 17.113	16 49.124
13	28 17.103	16 49.166
14	28 17.004	16 49.248
15	28 16.830	16 49.267
16	28 16.673	16 49.289
17	28 16.659	16 49.144
18	28 16.617	16 49.149
19	28 16.600	16 49.152
20	28 16.380	16 49.193
21	28 16.347	16 49.207
22	28 16.221	16 49.249
23	28 16.189	16 49.215
24	28 16.136	16 49.160

2.

AN OK CORRAL

Wp	N	W
1	28 17.140	16 48.719
2	28 17.160	16 48.807
3	28 17.161	16 48.830
4	28 17.149	16 48.856
5	28 17.152	16 48.864
6	28 17.241	16 48.968
7	28 17.270	16 49.023
8	28 17.236	16 49.048
9	28 17.254	16 49.123
10	28 17.248	16 49.214
11	28 17.149	16 49.317
12	28 17.167	16 49.404
13	28 17.161	16 49.476

3.

TRUE GRIT

Wp	N	W
1	28 15.991	16 49.003
2	28 15.874	16 48.966
3	28 15.873	16 48.936
4	28 15.836	16 48.914
5	28 15.821	16 48.879
6	28 15.798	16 48.864
7	28 15.633	16 48.702
8	28 15.607	16 48.703
9	28 15.592	16 48.698
10	28 15.602	16 48.660
11	28 15.828	16 48.449
12	28 15.854	16 48.373
13	28 15.875	16 48.357
14	28 16.026	16 48.374
15	28 16.049	16 48.393
16	28 16.088	16 48.480
17	28 16.129	16 48.543
18	28 16.324	16 48.441
19	28 16.501	16 48.404
20	28 16.728	16 48.298
21	28 16.844	16 48.341
22	28 16.719	16 48.485
23	28 16.774	16 48.647
24	28 16.809	16 48.713
25	28 16.786	16 48.779
26	28 16.762	16 48.805
27	28 16.681	16 48.833
28	28 16.646	16 48.836
29	28 16.538	16 48.846
30	28 16.354	16 48.862
31	28 16.320	16 48.885
32	28 16.256	16 48.977

4.

LASSO LA HOYA

Wp	N	W
1	28 16.049	16 48.393
2	28 16.150	16 48.458
3	28 16.162	16 48.471
4	28 16.176	16 48.479
5	28 16.211	16 48.445
6	28 16.225	16 48.406
7	28 16.230	16 48.438
8	28 16.287	16 48.402
9	28 16.335	16 48.391
10	28 16.295	16 48.380
11	28 16.388	16 48.203
12	28 16.252	16 48.211
13	28 16.195	16 48.186
14	28 16.132	16 48.294

5.

LAUREL & HARDY

Wp	N	W
1	28 18.997	16 48.194
2	28 18.963	16 48.246
3	28 18.936	16 48.378
4	28 18.951	16 48.387
5	28 18.951	16 48.402
6	28 18.983	16 48.417
7	28 18.958	16 48.493
8	28 18.981	16 48.576
9	28 19.010	16 48.774
10	28 19.083	16 48.810
11	28 19.062	16 48.834
12	28 18.897	16 48.998
13	28 18.895	16 49.212
14	28 18.836	16 49.224
15	28 18.807	16 49.220
16	28 18.724	16 49.136
17	28 18.712	16 49.079
18	28 18.783	16 49.004
19	28 18.696	16 49.069
20	28 18.638	16 48.838
21	28 18.717	16 48.308

6.

SADDLE UP AND ROUND THAT MOUNTAIN

Wp	N	W
1	28 18.096	16 48.879
2	28 18.165	16 49.043
3	28 18.197	16 49.087
4	28 18.319	16 49.196
5	28 18.409	16 49.269
6	28 18.426	16 49.354
7	28 18.419	16 49.404
8	28 18.423	16 49.417
9	28 18.323	16 49.475
10	28 18.295	16 49.502
11	28 18.729	16 49.536
12	28 18.744	16 49.522
13	28 18.744	16 49.505
14	28 18.719	16 49.314
15	28 18.721	16 49.086
16	28 18.702	16 49.076
17	28 18.642	16 48.846
18	28 18.716	16 48.308
19	28 18.699	16 48.298
20	28 18.669	16 48.310

21	28 18.612	16 48.282
22	28 18.511	16 48.146
23	28 18.491	16 48.150
24	28 18.364	16 48.281
25	28 18.315	16 48.345

7.

PICNIC AT HANGING ROCK + GUEGUE

1	28 17.931	16 49.494
2	28 17.867	16 49.555
3	28 17.828	16 49.685
4	28 17.835	16 49.767
5	28 17.835	16 49.806
6	28 17.761	16 49.960
7	28 17.734	16 50.019
8	28 17.718	16 50.048
9	28 17.706	16 50.112
10	28 17.692	16 50.129
11	28 17.676	16 50.168
12	28 17.656	16 50.199
13	28 17.666	16 50.211
14	28 17.581	16 50.255
15	28 17.589	16 50.277
16	28 17.585	16 50.300
17	28 17.584	16 50.316
18	28 17.556	16 50.358
19	28 17.593	16 50.367
20	28 17.567	16 50.402
21	28 17.550	16 50.436
22	28 17.522	16 50.473

From Agriculture To Tourism

Before tourism became its most important industry, much of the south of Tenerife was a patchwork of plantations and *fincas*. The hotels and apartments of the resorts stand on land once painstakingly terraced, producing a variety of crops including bananas, tomatoes and grapes. Terrace walls hand-built from rock, stones and boulders served a dual purpose; they made the steep volcanic slopes more workable, and they helped prevent the erosion of precious top soil.

Then there was the problem of irrigation to solve. It might seem at first glance that the island, especially the south, must be seriously short of water, but though the rainfall on the coastal areas is low there is plenty of precipitation at higher altitudes. The farmers therefore built a network of water channels to run across the surface of the land.

From the 1960s, tourism began to take on importance in the south, and its growth has continued steadily. For all the criticism that is sometimes levelled at this rapid expansion, tourism has provided many much-needed jobs and has, on balance, been good for the island. But one result has been the loss of agriculture. Although commercial scale banana plantations are still found in the south, the attractions of a job in tourism leave the hard life of wresting a living from the land a poor second choice for many Canarians.

The remnants of terracing are still visible on the slopes, and sections of the irrigation system remain. A few still carry water. Even where the original open canals are disused, modern pipe work often runs alongside these old systems, confirming that these old waterways were built along the most logical routes. You will see many examples of terracing and water canals on a number of walks in this book, often in seemingly inaccessible places.

Plant Life

Even the *malpais* areas of the south, which seem to consist of rough, naked lava rock, support plant life. The area covered by the walks in this book takes in a wide variety of species, from the desert plants adapted to harsh, hot almost soil-free areas, to the pine forests. The *barrancos* explored on our walks are often filled with lush flowering plants, many unique to Tenerife (for example, Walk

Photo opportunity - Roque del Conde in the background, ancient and modern water systems in the foreground providing moisture for lush plant life including *Lavandula canariensis*. (Walk 13, Fantasia)

2, 'Barranco del Infierno'), and the phenomenon of the bramble-choked *barranco* seen on Walk 9, 'Taucho Tour' is, in our experience, unique. The mountain slopes which face the moist onshore winds are studded with

Common in Tenerife, the cardón or Candelabra Cactus (*Euphorbia canariensis*).

strange, endemic succulents, while ancient almond trees, olives, Canarian palms and figs have established themselves in the more fertile pockets.

As for cultivated plant life; you will see grape vines, potatoes, tomatoes, oranges, lemons, avocados and papaya growing in village gardens, and many ornamental plants including hibiscus and bougainvillea (for example, Walk 12, 'Walkers Who Lunch') and on the fertile upland fields in the **Ifonche** area (Walk 10, 'Wow! Spectacular' and Walk 11, 'Queen Of The South').

Wildlife

Wild rabbits thrive on Tenerife, and you may see wild goats while following our walks, while a few *cabreros* still tend herds of goats, even as close to mass tourism as **Mount Guaza** and the **Guaza Plateau**, on Walk 3, 'Barren Grandeur' or Walk 4, 'Mount Guaza'. Bird lovers will have more to watch out for although these are more often heard than seen, with the exception of birds of prey which cruise the slopes, and the Hoopoe (*Upapa epops*) with its distinctive black and white wings. Various species of gulls and sea birds including the Sandwich Tern (*Sterna sandvicensis*) the Herring Gull (*Larus Argentatus*) will accompany you on coastal routes such as Walk 5, 'Coastal Escapism', or Walk 1, 'Life In The Raw'. Lizards of various species are easier to spot, as are butterflies in sizes from thumbnail to hand-sized. Other insect life that you are likely to spot while walking includes several species of bees, dragonflies, moths, beetles (look out for the cochineal beetles in their protective coating of white dust which colonise prickly pear cacti), and spiders.

You rarely see two goats with similar colouring.

SOUTHERN WALKS LOCATOR MAP

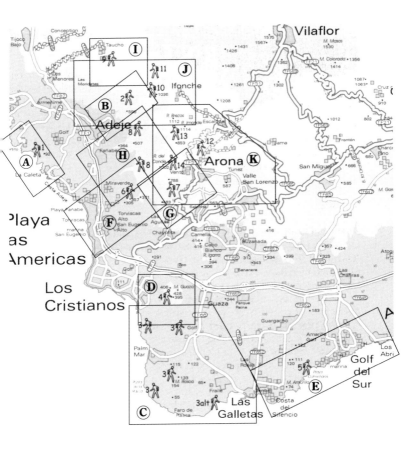

1. LIFE IN THE RAW

This walk leaves tourism behind and heads off into countryside, providing an excellent introduction to the rugged southern landscapes. Our route begins in **La Caleta** and follows coastal paths, taking in the hippie colony at **Spaghetti Beach**, beaches and *barrancos* before reaching our half way point at **El Puertito**, where we take a break, then returning with variations to our start point.

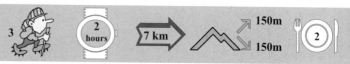

3 | 2 hours | 7 km | 150m / 150m | 2

Our start point is in the village of **La Caleta**, just inland from the sea at the cross roads on **Calle Las Artes** where we head west (**Wp.1, W**) on the new road and past a roundabout, then going right onto a dirt road before taking the steep rock path up the ridge, the stone drumming from our footfalls, aiming for the signboard visible on the ridge. We reach the ridge (**Wp.2, 6M**) and step through a low stone wall, passing two *Espacio Naturaleza Protegido* signs, our manicured dirt path running ahead, other paths running left and right from the signs. At another junction of paths running seawards and inland (**Wp.3, 8M**), we have a choice of routes into **Hippie Valley**; ahead is the steeper route, while we take the right hand option marked as suitable for wheelchairs!

Once named Spaghetti Beach in the days when an Italian naturist chef cooked here, wearing only a sea captain's cap, this 'alternative' valley is dotted with hippie shacks of rock boulders and palm fronds, and tepees. The path runs around the valley giving us an arms' length view of the natural lifestyle, crossing the valley's watercourse (**Wp.4, 10M**), on a stone-laid section before it runs gently down to meet the shorter route (**Wp.5, 13M**).

Our path climbs gently before starting a steep ascent of the valley's western wall. Just before the top of our climb (**Wp.6, 18M**), a path goes left as we continue up to a marker post at a junction of paths (**Wp.7**). Continuing ahead, we cross the high ground and begin dropping down into *barranco* country, waves breaking far below us as we descend on the well-made trail to more hippie encampments in the *barranco*. This large cove is formed by three *barrancos* meeting the sea, giving rise to interesting geological formations.

We cross the *barranco* watercourse (**Wp.8, 23M**) and climb gently uphill, staying on the main path and ignoring side paths off to camping areas. Over the headland between the two *barrancos* by a blue tepee (**Wp.9, 27M**), our path is now stone over rock, heading towards long-abandoned plantations on the far side of the second *barranco*. We begin to drop into the second *barranco* (**Wp.10**), the path much less clear now until it crosses the watercourse (**Wp.11, 31M**). As we ascend we come onto a clearer path which meanders along to the remains of an old dirt road, becoming concrete as it climbs (**Wp.12**) towards an abandoned plantation. The concrete comes to an end (**Wp.13, 34M**) and we drop into another small *barranco* before climbing rock sheets to come up to a dirt road around the old plantation (**Wp.14, 36M**). We follow the dirt road inland, running up into the valley past abandoned

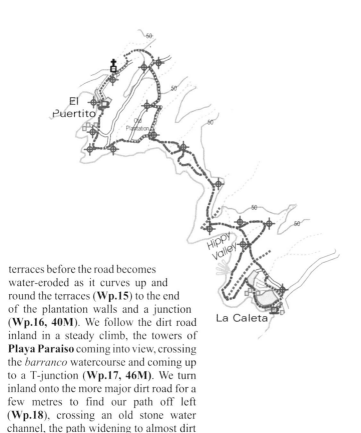

terraces before the road becomes water-eroded as it curves up and round the terraces (**Wp.15**) to the end of the plantation walls and a junction (**Wp.16, 40M**). We follow the dirt road inland in a steady climb, the towers of **Playa Paraiso** coming into view, crossing the *barranco* watercourse and coming up to a T-junction (**Wp.17, 46M**). We turn inland onto the more major dirt road for a few metres to find our path off left (**Wp.18**), crossing an old stone water channel, the path widening to almost dirt road width and curving into the *barranco* with **El Puertito** on our left.

The path swings left to an electricity pylon (**Wp.19**) and a path runs along the spur of bare rock before becoming indistinct. We continue down the spur to lose height before we need to leave the ridge and scramble down the rocks and stone slopes (**Wp.20**) to meet an old dirt road at the back of the village (**Wp.21, 57M**) which takes us to **El Puertito's** small church and parking area (**Wp.22**), to step onto the tarmac road curving down to the sea front of **El Puertito** and **Pepe y Lola's** little bar (**Wp.23, 63M**).

After refreshment we begin our return (**0M**) by walking in front of the bar and following the path which wriggles between the jumble of houses to climb out of the bay and onto a headland where we pick up the coastal path. We cross a dirt road (**Wp.24, 5M**) and continue on the coastal route, passing another *Espacio Natureleza Protegido* signpost with no board (**Wp.25**) as we head towards the old plantation that we skirted on the outward route.

Our route widens to a dirt road taking us to the edge of the *barranco* (**Wp.26**) and onto a path which descends to its floor, crossing it on an old stone wall and climbing up towards the banana plantation on the next headland, heading towards its nearest corner where rock steps take us up to the level of the plantation and a dirt road.

Following the dirt road right, we meet our outward route (**Wp.14**) and retrace our steps across the *barranco* before descending the concrete and dirt road. This time we walk along the pebble foreshore to climb/scramble up onto the headland. Before reaching our outward route (at **Wp.9**) we take a path above the sea, waves crashing on interesting rock formations, before dropping down to the sea and its 'cossie-optional' beach suitable for bathing.

Climbing away from the 'beach', our path wriggles up the slopes to join our main path (our outward route, **Wp.27, 26M**). We retrace our route down the steep path into **Hippie Valley** but this time we take the short route across the valley (**Wp.5**). After the valley's impressive watercourse, we face a steep climb up the eastern wall, back to the junction of paths (**Wp.3**).

This time we turn right for an easy stroll seawards with dramatic views over **Hippie Valley** and its cove, the views becoming even more impressive as our path comes to the cliff edge (take care) before the route swings left (**Wp.28**) We come to a low stone wall (**Wp.29**) where a path goes left to **Wp.2**. Through the wall, our path runs inland to the rear of new apartments (**Wp.30**). You could take a quick route back to our start point, but we turn right to drop down the wide stairs to ground level, where we go right to the second bay of **La Caleta**. A path leads through the houses to the sea front bar, from where we head up the narrow road past a fish restaurant on our right to the crossroads at our start point.

2. BARRANCO DEL INFIERNO

Behind the county town of **Adeje** is Tenerife's most popular walk - the **Barranco del Infierno**. Local legend says the gorge is so deep the sun never reaches the bottom, and while this is unlikely to be true the 'barranco architecture' of the walk should not be missed. Easy access by bus (416, 441 or 473) from **Los Cristianos** and **Playa de las Américas**. This walk is extremely popular so we advise an early start and avoid weekends. (You may find that there is a small charge of about three euros at the entrance to the walk on week days.)

3   2.5 hours   7 km   180m   180m   3

Taking the bus from the resort, ask for **Barranco del Infierno**, and get off at the highest stop in **Adeje**; the town's expansion now means that you will have a bit of an uphill walk past the Town Hall (*Ayuntamiento*) and church to go left to the cannon outside **Villa de Adeje** and follow the road round to the right. A very steep climb takes you up to **Otello's** (closed Tuesdays) and the walk starts directly behind the restaurant (**Wp.1, 0M**). Car parking can be a problem close to **Otello's** and you may have to park at the bottom of the steep hill.

After that steep climb to the official start of Tenerife's most 'manicured' and popular walk, you can rest up on the shaded seating before setting off down the stone-laid track behind **Otello's**. The trail clings to the northern face of the *barranco* for the first half of our journey (**30-45M**). Although the path has been levelled and edged, with stairs for ascents and descents, it is still an energetic walk. Our route hugs the cliff face and so has excellent views, though the precipitous drops at the edge of the path might disturb vertigo sufferers. There are several turns with viewing points along this first section for those essential photographs, or for just taking a breather; (**Wp.2, 9M**) viewing platform, (**Wp.3**) crossing the watercourse in the side **Barranco Chavon**, (**Wp.4, 15M**) spectacularly sited viewing platform, (**Wp.5**) cross working canal on small bridge, (**Wps.6 & 7**) viewing platforms.

Just about the time you're thinking this is a 'nice' walk with great views but are wondering why people say it is 'spectacular', the trail leads down into the *barranco*. We drop down to cross the water canal on another log bridge (**Wp.8**) and come down to a wooden bridge over the *barranco*'s watercourse (**Wp.9, 33M**). From here the nature of our walk changes as we follow the stream along the floor of the canyon. Now we are in close contact with the plants of Tenerife, but please do not pick flowers or uproot plants as this is a protected area.

Reaching **La Cojedra** (**Wp.10, 39M** and well signed), you may think that this cliff face represents the famous waterfall, but the water pipes leading along the path show there is still some way to go. **La Cojedra** makes a pleasant resting point before tackling the final stage. A water canal tumbles invitingly

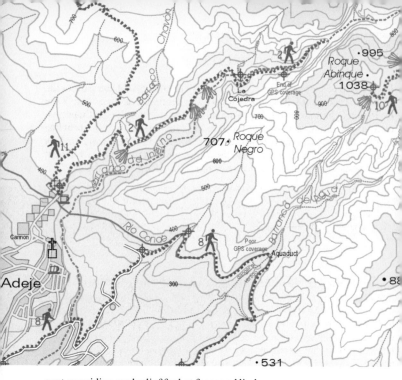

past, providing cool relief for hot faces and limbs.

The path after **La Cojedra** is hemmed in by bushes, while cliffs close over us as we criss-cross the stream on bridges (**Wps.11, 12 and 13**); after which we lose any GPS signal due to the sheer-sided *barranco*. As we progress the 'Barranco Architecture' becomes increasingly spectacular, with the path leading us alongside the stream, and criss-crossing it, beneath the towering heights. Only at the very end does the path peter out leaving us with a scramble over rocks before turning the last corner. Hidden until the last few metres of the walk, the waterfall is very impressive as it cascades 100 metres down the sheer face of the *barranco* into a still pool. For this sight alone the **Barranco del Infierno** should be included in everyone's itinerary of Southern Tenerife.

There is no way up and over the *barranco,* so we return by retracing our steps, including the stiff climb up from the *barranco* floor.

Otello's (closed Tuesdays) at the end of the walk is the logical, and nearest, place for refreshment. Sitting in the restaurant you can enjoy the view down over **Adeje** to the coast, or a view up into the *barranco* from their rear terrace, while tucking into the local speciality - Garlic Chicken (Pollo al Ajillo). **Adeje** has several good value bar/restaurants including **Oasis** and **La Rambla** below the town hall with another couple of *tipicos* across the road. Garlic chicken is the local speciality and is available in most bar/restaurants.

As **Barranco del Infierno** is the most popular walk in Tenerife, it is best to begin early if you want to avoid the crowds. A 9.30 start gives the best conditions, avoids most of the crowds, and you can finish the walk with lunch.

3. BARREN GRANDEUR

Deserts and deserted coastlines have a beauty all their own. Here we tour the 'Barren Grandeur' of the **Guaza Plateau** and deserted coastline out to **Faro de Rasca** lighthouse, returning by an inland route. From the lighthouse we also have an alternative route to finish in **Las Galletas**, with its frequent bus service back to **Los Cristianos**. Starting from the southern end of **Los Cristianos** we are immediately into the desert, with very limited refreshment opportunities, which assumes its own beauty when seen at close quarters.

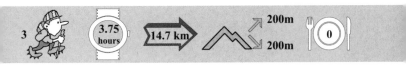

3   3.75 hours   14.7 km   200m / 200m   0

Starting from the **Costamar Apartments** at the southern end of **Los Cristianos (Wp.1, 0M),** we follow the tarmac lane down to a walled villa to swing left and follow the beach path along to an *Espacio Naturaleza Protegido* sign (**Wp.2**), where we climb up onto a path to start zigzagging up the cliffs. Alternatively, walk along in front of new villas to new stone steps and climb up a path to the traditional route. Our well-marked path gets rougher as we climb, passing a new path coming in from the left (**Wp.3**) and the surface changes from dirt to broken rock, until the route turns into a cleft (**Wp.4, 13M**) approximately half way up the cliffs; if you look towards **Los Cristianos** at this point, you will be facing directly towards the **Princesa Dacil Hotel**.

We take a faint path which climbs away from the main walking route (**SW**) to pass a small cave (**Wp.5, 16M**) as we climb above our earlier route, and our path becomes more defined. Up through a hairpin

Looking north from the Guaza plateau.

bend, we continue up into the plateau to go over a crest and meander into a shallow valley to a T-junction with another path (**Wp.6, 23M**). We go right (**SW**) to follow the path over to the *parapente* launch point on a bald knoll (**Wp.7**) marked by tattered wind flags. We go **SW** on a path which drops into a *barranco*, and then climb its southern side back up onto the plateau to curve around the cliffs before turning into a valley (**Wp.8, 30M**), where our path contours round to cross the watercourse and bring us back above the sea. Our path wanders through a landscape of tumbled valleys (**SSW**) which drop into the sea on our right until we meet a larger *barranco*. Small shale heaps show that this was a stone cutting area, as we head inland past a shattered rock before crossing the *barranco* floor (**Wp.9, 35M**) and heading seawards. Before reaching the sea, our route swings left (**S**) into a small valley littered with shale heaps. Cresting a small rise, we see a large stone quarry on the far side of a valley. We curve left to descend into the valley and cross the stream bed (**Wp.10, 40M**) below a second quarry.

Although the main path leads off to the further quarry, we look for a path on our left (**Wp.11**) which climbs up alongside this quarry to become clearer when we are upon the plateau. Now it is easy strolling (**SSE**) past a path off to the left (**Wp.12, 44M**) by the remains of a cairn, for us to come to the top of the cliffs (**Wp.13**) overlooking **La Arenita** beach. In a few metres we meet a path coming from the plateau on our left (**Wp.14**), and a small quarry is on our right at the top of the cliffs. On the path, we go right and left past a substantial cairn, to start descending the wall of a valley. This is an adventurous descent, and care is needed due to the loose stones which litter the generally well-made path. We wind down the wall of this sharp valley towards the beach, our route taking to bare rock where a section of path has fallen away (**Wp.15**). The path drops steeply down below a burnt orange rock outcrop for an almost scrambling descent before our route runs out into a tumbled landscape to a '*pa*' sign (**Wp.16**). We swing down an old dirt road to arrive on a dirt road which runs alongside the large pebble beach. Turning left, we are just an easy stroll away from the seaward face of **Palm Mar** (**60M**). If you want to take a break at this point, head inland onto the 'main' road, and behind the **Trattoria** restaurant you will find **Bar Super**, a modern version of a rustic *tipico* for snacks and drinks.

PALM MAR TO FARO DE RASCA

On the seaward side of **Palm Mar** (**0M**) we head **SSW** along a dirt road to come onto a new road by the **Playa La Arenita** beach sign (**Wp.17, 10M**). In a few metres the broad new road swings left so we go right onto a coastal track (**Wp.18**) to go over a jagged volcanic point and undulate along the lava coastline (**S**) passing narrow dirt roads off to our left (**Wp.19, 15M**) and (**Wp.20, 17M**), until the dirt road finishes (**Wp.21**), for us to continue on a narrow path which comes onto a small flood plain with a boulder wall on its seaward side (**Wp.22**). Towards the end of the wall, we step through a tumbled section onto a dirt road that runs down to the sea. Looking left (**S**) we spot the narrow coastal walking trail threading its way through the volcanic boulders, with the sea breaking on the lava shoreline on our right.

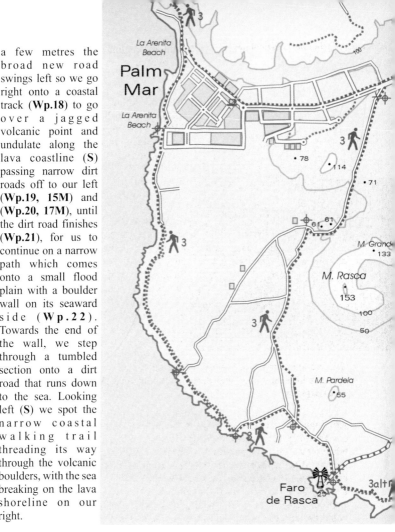

Our faint trail twists along through the surreal landscape with a substantial boulder wall 50m inland of us as we cross a dirt road and come to a '*pa*' sign above a pocket in the shoreline (**Wp.23, 30M**). A boulder with a red bull's-eye marks our path's continuation through the *malpais* past rock shelters and a pair of foaming inlets. Across a sandy area, we continue amongst tumbled lava and over a ridge crowned with rock shelters which overlooks a pretty bay. Our route is **SSW** to crest another ridge and come to a junction overlooking another picturesque bay (**44M**).

Now we head inland on a rough rock road (**Wp.24**) onto a flood plain (**Wp.25**). We follow the dirt road heading inland to a junction of dirt roads (**Wp.26**). Keeping straight on, we cross another junction (**Wp.27**) and pass another dirt road off to our left (**Wp.28**) before our route climbs up to join the *faro*'s tarmac access road (**Wp.29**) for us to stroll the few metres to the **Faro de Rasca** (**Wp.30, 55M**). The lighthouse area is a pleasant spot to take a break overlooking the *malpais* and volcanic bays pounded by the Atlantic Ocean.

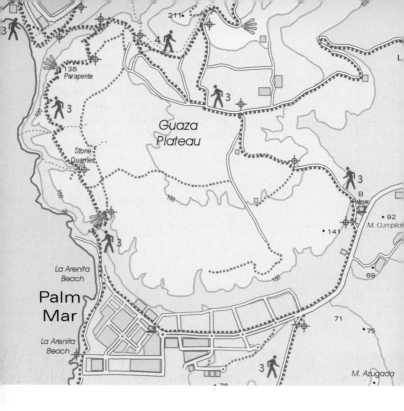

FARO DE RASCA TO LOS CRISTIANOS

Refreshed (**0M**), we retrace our route down into the *malpais* until we come to the second dirt road junction (**Wp.27**) where we go right (**N**). At the end of the dirt road where it turns back on itself (**Wp.31**), we cut across the open *malpais* (**NW**) to strike a dirt road (**Wp.32**) for us to head **N**. Past dirt roads off to our left (**Wps.33 & 34**), our dirt road curves around **Montaña Rasca** with a low stone wall on our right. It is easy strolling across the plain, passing more dirt roads off to our left (**Wps.35 & 36**) before we come up to a T-junction (**Wp.37**).

Going right, we start climbing on the rough road to pass a '*pa*' sign (**Wp.38, 25M**) and continue ascending between red hills before curving left to cross a gentle plain ringed by small hills. Our road climbs gently up through a pass in the red hills to drop into a second plain with a fruit plantation away on our right. A second gentle climb through a second pass brings us up to overlook the **Palm Mar** road and a gentle stroll down past the locked vehicle barrier (**Wp.39, 37M**).

We walk inland on the tarmac passing a walled bungalow, to just before **El Palmar** where we find an old dirt road marked by a '*pa*' sign (**Wp.40, 47M**) which climbs up onto the **Guaza Plateau**. The chain barrier by the '*pa*' sign is superfluous as the road has eroded to the stage of being impassable to vehicles. It is a hard slog up what remains of the road to climb above the restaurant and banana plantations as we curve towards the west

A large cairn (**Wp.41**) marks the end of the main climb as the gradient moderates to bring us up onto the plateau (**Wp.42, 63M**). Here, by a small cairn, we step through a tumbled wall onto a walking trail lined with stones, to come onto a dirt road (**Wp.43**). Our dirt road curves towards **Mount Guaza** (**N**) bringing us up to a T-junction below the farm (**Wp.44**) where we go left (**W**). When the main dirt road goes right (**Wp.45**) we continue straight ahead on a dirt road which curves round abandoned terraces. After descending gently, the dirt road swings left (**Wp.46, 82M**) as we continue ahead on a walking trail to come onto the main path up from **Los Cristianos**. Once on the main path, it is all downhill - not that this is a relaxing section as the loose rocks littering the route demand care for every step. Halfway down the cliff face, we meet our outward route to retrace our step back to the **Costamar Apartments**, 105 minutes (**105M**) from **Faro de Rasca**.

ALTERNATIVE FINISH - FARO DE RASCA TO LAS GALLETAS

This route forms a section of our coastal route which links to **Las Galletas** and the start of our **Los Abrigos** route. This section starts well but becomes uninspiring, so look forward to the sea front restaurants.

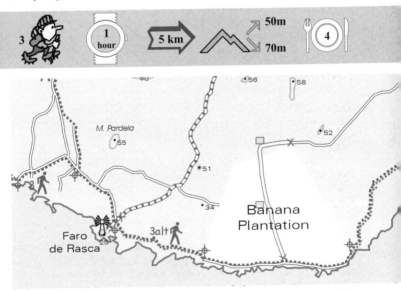

To the east (**E**) of the *faro* is a huge covered banana plantation, and our first target is the seaward corner of this great tented structure. From **Faro de Rasca** we walk to the vehicle barrier on the tarmac lane and swing right (**Wp.1**) down a rough sloping track.

From the bottom of the slope, a faint walking trail meanders eastwards (**E**) through the rocks before climbing up to a '*pa*' sign post, at which point we drop down onto a broad dirt road on the seaward corner of the plantation

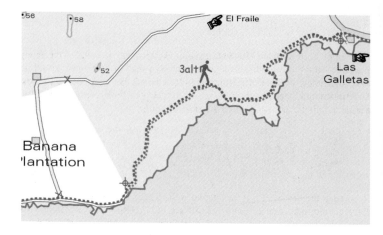

(**Wp.2**). We stroll (**E**) between the massive foundations of the plantations and an impressive rocky coastline for over a kilometre, passing a tarmac plantation road (**Wp.3**) before coming to the end of the dirt road and plantation (**Wp.4**). We squeeze around a palm tree to enter an area of *malpais* where agriculture was abandoned decades ago.

We head north-east (**NE**) to pass the crumbling walls of old plantations on our left (**Wp.5**) and then on our right, before swinging east-north-east (**ENE**) to pass an old water channel on our left (**Wp.6**). The *malpais* is featureless although confused by a myriad of dirt tracks. Keeping the town of **El Fraile** on our left, we head approximately east (**E**) to **Wp.9**, although our own route passes through **Wp.7** and then through **Wp.8** to look across to the red doors of the **Cruz Roja** (Red Cross) building. Walking trails take us past little bays and unofficial camping areas to reach the **Cruz Roja** car park (**Wp10**). We now have an easy stroll along the pavement to **Las Galletas** for refreshments in one of the sea front restaurants.

LINK FROM LAS GALLETAS TO THE START OF THE LOS ABRIGOS ROUTE

Walk east (**E**) through **Las Galletas** to come onto the main road heading north (**Wp.11**). Head inland, then turn off at the **Ten Bel Commercial Centre** (**Wp.12**), to walk east (**E**) and then north (**N**) to the **Chapparal Commercial Centre** with its totem poles (**Wp.13**). Continue east (**E**), passing **Chayofita** on your left and coming to the traffic island (**Wp.14**). From this point, choose either to go left then right, or right then left, to reach the alternative start points of the route to **Los Abrigos**, Walk 5, 'Coastal Escapism'.

4. MOUNT GUAZA

Seen from the motorway, **Mount Guaza** appears inaccessible and so it is from the north - but our route takes us up from the **Guaza Plateau** on an easy, but very strenuous, climb to the summit (428 metres). Being so close to **Los Cristianos**, and 'because it is there', many people climb to the summit by accident; unbelievable once you have done it, but true.

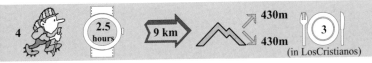

4   2.5 hours   9 km   430m / 430m   3 (in LosCristianos)

We start at the new walking trail between the **Playa Graciosa** and **Paradise Park** developments on the edge of **Los Cristianos (Wp.1, 0M)** by taking the steps down into the water runoff and set off on the nicely manicured path for a gentle stroll up to join the traditional walking trail **(Wp.2, 3M)**.

Turning uphill, we start climbing seriously up through a zigzag, the path getting rougher while **Los Cristianos** gets smaller, for us to pass the turn off of our **Palm Mar** route **(Wp.3, 8M)**. The going gets rougher as we come to a tempting path straight ahead **(Wp.4, 13M)** where we climb right on the main path. We keep climbing with our route swinging right to follow the *barranco* and pass paths off to our right **(Wps.5 & 6)** before coming to the junction **(Wp.7, 16M)** with our return from **Faro de Rasca** route.

Here we continue straight on, thankfully gradient free, beside an old water channel along the lip of the *barranco* until our path starts climbing up through the tumbled walls of old terraces **(Wp.8)** before returning to the *barranco*'s lip. More climbing up through old terraces, including a section where the path splits in two **(Wp.9)** before rejoining, brings us up to the end of an old dirt road **(Wp.10, 21M)**. We swing left to walk up a path facing the intimidating bulk of the mountain, with the *barranco* dropping away on our left, to slog our way up to join the **Mount Guaza** dirt road **(Wp.11, 27M)**.

If you thought it was energetic so far - well, now it gets tougher as we slog up the wide and dusty dirt road, passing an old walking trail on our left before passing the vehicle barrier **(Wp.12)**. The road swings right after the barrier for us to climb up to a hairpin bend with panoramic views, **Los Palos Golf** standing out like an emerald jewel amongst the dull, tented banana plantations.

After a break for the views it is back to slogging uphill with hills on our right, a *barranco* on our left and a seemingly endless ascent ahead on the dusty road. Cresting a rise **(Wp.13, 39M)** we have a short section of downhill before the ascent is rejoined. Finally the tops of aerials come into view as we walk up to a junction **(Wp.14, 56M)** where a new dirt road sweeps left around the *caldera*. Straight ahead, we climb up the old road to pass a large cairn **(Wp.15)** and then a final steep slog brings us up to the Trig point amongst the old transmitters **(Wp.16, 63M)**.

Technically this is the top of our route, but not the end as after a break to

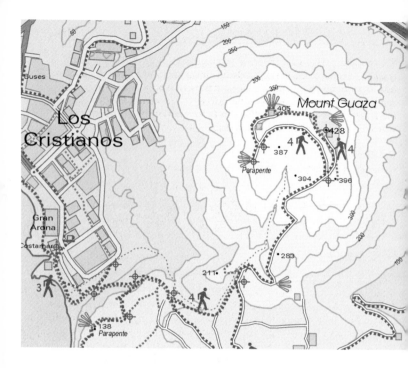

recover we continue down the old jeep trail (**0M**) to come down to the second
set of transmitters (**Wp.17**) for views over **Playa de Las Américas**. Now it is
easy strolling along the new dirt road past the newest transmitters and down to
a junction (**Wp.18**) where we go out to a *parapente* launch point for views
over **Los Cristianos (Wp.19)** and our start point way below us.

Back on the dirt road an easy stroll and gentle uphill bring us back to the
junction with our outward route (**Wp.14, 20M**). Now it is all downhill (!)
remembering to take as much care on the descent as the ascent, particularly on
the very rough path down from the plateau, and we are back at our start point
after **145 minutes,** including a 17 minute break (to recover) at the Trig point.

5. COASTAL ESCAPISM

This coastal walk is deceptively interesting, with its dramatic coastline quite in contrast to the boring landscape inland from our route. A good hike to work up an appetite for lunch in the **Los Abrigos** seafood restaurants, or as an escape from the golf developments; take your choice, but it is tougher than it looks. You can finish the walk at **Los Abrigos**, in which case time and distance are approximately halved.

Full Route
(halve time, distance, ascents & descents if finishing in **Los Abrigos**)

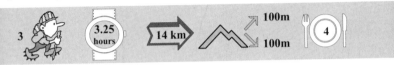

3 | 3.25 hours | 14 km | 100m / 100m | 4

Choose your starting point

Our start point in **Costa del Silencio** depends on the sea conditions. If the sea is turbulent we start at **Coral Mar (Wpt.1A)** and walk across to the *Espacio Naturaleza Protegido* sign to follow a clear path alongside a wall around the base of **Montaña Amarilla** which undulates gently along, passing a path off right **(Wpt.2A)**. We continue until we come just above a barrier to our left on a dirt road **(Wpt.3A)**, where we head downhill and seawards, passing a junction of dirt roads **(Wpt.4A)** while looking for another *Espacio Naturaleza Protegido* sign down on our left **(Wpt.5A)**. This marks the 'official' path which we reach in the maze of dirt roads and paths in this confused area **(Wpt.8, 12M)**.

When the sea is quiet and at low tide, we start off from the pebble beach below **Chasna** to follow the shoreline around the rocks below **Montaña Amarilla**. We pass an *Espacio Naturaleza Protegido* sign and **Montaña Amarilla** on the left **(Wpt.1, 4M)**, and begin to negotiate the rocks (popular with naturists at weekends and holidays, so watch where you put those boots), taking care as they are slippery.

The slippery rocks end **(Wpt.2, 9M)** and we climb a slope of rock to ascend onto the headland, where we find the coastal path **(Wpt.3, 16M)** which winds around between the impressive coastline and the *malpais* inland, before dropping down to the "pa" sign in a gully.

Once on the official path, route finding is easy. We pass a junction of paths (**Wpt.4**) where a staired route climbs **Montaña Amarilla** and another route goes left as we continue along the coast. A path runs off right to run around the headland (**Wpt.5, 18M**) as our walking trail meanders through this *malpais* landscape with the rugged coastline on our right, passing another cross roads of paths (**Wpt.6, 20M**). Now **Amarilla Golf, Golf del Sur** and **Los Abrigos** come into view ahead. A path runs back left towards **Montaña Amarilla** (**Wpt.7, 24M**) as we join our alternative starting point (**Wpt.8**) near a '*pa*' sign.

Yet another start is to climb **Montaña Amarilla** (steeper than it looks, and dangerous if windy) to the summit and then follow the right hand path around the rim of the *caldera* before dropping down and heading seawards to pick up the coastal path.

The onward route

A dirt track comes in from the left (**Wpt.9, 29M**), and then vegetation begins, with *tabaiba* and prickly pear each side of the path (**Wpt.10, 31M**). Our path turns inland into a pebble dunes area (**Wpt.11, 35M**) with a pebble 'alps' inland, as we come down towards the bay of **Playa Colmenares**.

Wild, unspoilt views on 'Coastal Escapism'.

It is a wobbly walk across the pebbles to come onto a dirt road which drops us down behind the beach with a dirt road coming in from the left (**Wpt.12, 44M**). Following the road, or wobbly walking along the pebble beach, brings us to the end of the bay where we head between the sea and a lagoon to pick up the **Amarilla Golf** coastal path (**Wpt.13, 47M**).

This well made path has the steepest ascents and descents of the whole route as it runs along the impressive coastline at the edge of the golf development. We pass a dirt road (**Wpt. 14**) which runs left into **Amarilla Golf** as we continue on the coastal path, passing the 5th tee (**Wpt.15**) on the left. The path takes us past apartments and a road off on our left (**Wpt.16, 52M**) and then a path left (**Wpt.17**), which short cuts the ridge after waypoint 16 before running out at the entrance to the marina (**Wpt.18, 64M**).

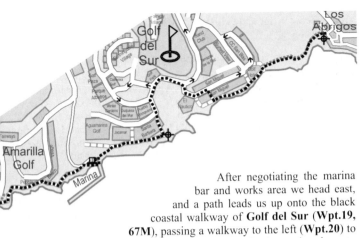

After negotiating the marina bar and works area we head east, and a path leads us up onto the black coastal walkway of **Golf del Sur** (**Wpt.19, 67M**), passing a walkway to the left (**Wpt.20**) to stroll along past the **Santa Barbara** timeshare to follow the black path inland (**Wpt.21, 72M**) for us to come up to a road junction (**Wpt.22**). We go right, turning onto **Calle San Miguel** and into **San Miguel** with **El Nautico** on our right (**Wpt.23**) and taking a footpath onto the sea front walkway (**Wpt.24, 80M**).

A pleasant stroll along this impressive sea front brings us to the **Golf Hotel** (**Wpt.25, 85M**) and a road off left to **San Blas Centro Comercial**. Our path runs around the seaward side of the hotel, the end of **Golf del Sur**, for a staired descent to **Playa San Blas** (**Wpt.26**). We stroll down behind the pebbles before the path climbs out of the valley with a lagoon on our right (**Wpt.27, 90M**) and **Los Abrigos** ahead.

Across the headland, we have a semi-staired descent to the beach before ascending on a paved walkway to the edge of **Los Abrigos** (**Wpt.28, 97M**) where we have a choice of bars and restaurants for refreshments. If you would prefer to ride back, regular bus services run between **Los Abrigos** and the resorts of **Costa del Silencio**, **Los Cristianos** and **Playa de las Américas**.

Our return to **Los Cristianos** follows the same route, but as we approach **Montaña Amarilla** we have the alternative of following the base of the mountain on its inland (**N**) side. To take this alternative route, at the end of the dirt road leaving the *protegido* area marked by the signpost (**Wpt.5A**) we begin to turn inland, passing a junction of dirt roads (**Wpt.4A**).

Just before a gate across the dirt road we take an easy path which runs around the base of the mountain (**Wpt.3A**), ignoring a path off left (**Wpt.2A**) which runs into the *caldera*. As we enter the buildings of **Costa del Silencio**, we leave the path round the mountain near the **Chasna** building (**Wpt.1A**) to walk the few metres south (**S**) back to our start point (**3H 15M**).

6. PICOS LAS AMÉRICAS

In **Playa de las Américas**, the mountains are on your doorstep - actually, your back doorstep, as our energetic but most rewarding route reveals. This route also links with the **TS-11**, giving options to continue on to **Adeje** (Walk 8) or **Arona** (Walk 7), 'Down To Town'.

The geology is interesting, but the demands of the final section make it suitable for experienced mountain walkers only.

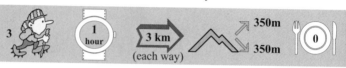

3   1 hour   3 km (each way)   350m / 350m   0

Town Section

Starting from the busy **San Eugenio** roundabout, we walk up the street heading inland past the **Las Dalias Hotel (Wp.1)**, to cross the motorway to a T-junction **(Wp.2, 5M)**. Going right in 50 metres, we turn onto a broad tiled path **(Wp.3)** to climb steeply up between the **Vista Mar** and **Roque Villas** developments, to arrive breathless back on **Avenida Europa (Wp.4)**. A steady uphill stroll takes us onto **Calle Suecia (Wp.5)** and up to another wide, steep, staired ascent **(Wp.6)**, for us to emerge at the **Calle Portugal** junction **(Wp.7, 15M)**. Now it is onwards and upwards as we slog up **Avenida Europa** to turn right **(Wp.8)** just before **Ocean View** for the last slog up to the ridge road **(Wp.9, 20M)**.

After the steep ascent, we are rewarded by an easy stroll towards the **Picos (W)** which are dramatically silhouetted against the bulk of **Roque del Conde** (Walk 14). There are sweeping views down over **Playa de las Américas** on our left, and the banana-filled *caldera* on our right, passing roads off to the left **(Wps. 10&11)** as we come up to the parking area **(Wp.12, 25M)**. Car users could cut out the energetic climbs by driving up to this point, so for the mountains section of the route we take the times from the car parking area.

Picos Section

Due to the exposed nature of the route, it should not be attempted in windy weather.

From the end of the tarmac **(Wp.1, 0M)**, a track leads around a water tank before narrowing to a walking trail which climbs steeply up to **The Pimple** (259 metres, **Wp.2, 8M**). Take particular care in ascending and descending **The Pimple**. The grit-covered nature of the route can result in the rock becoming slippery, and can easily upset the unwary. After taking in the panoramic views, we stroll down to the saddle to begin ascending the first peak. Soon after the start of the climb, we need to swing left at a junction marked by a cairn **(Wp.3)** to continue steeply upwards.

The path up to the first peak is not always clear, but if in doubt, climb up towards the highest point that you can see. The steep ascent eases as we come alongside the peak **(Wp.4, 14M)**, from which point a short scramble takes us up to the 350 metre high rock platform.

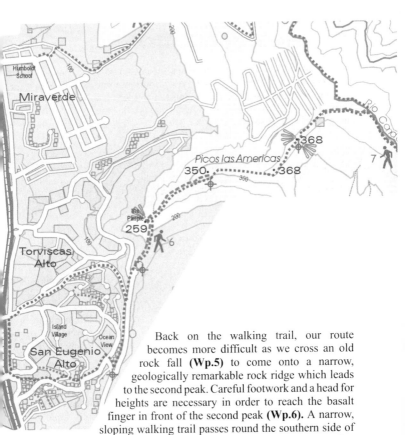

Back on the walking trail, our route becomes more difficult as we cross an old rock fall **(Wp.5)** to come onto a narrow, geologically remarkable rock ridge which leads to the second peak. Careful footwork and a head for heights are necessary in order to reach the basalt finger in front of the second peak **(Wp.6)**. A narrow, sloping walking trail passes round the southern side of the peak (once again - careful footwork is needed), to bring us to another ridge; an easy stroll this time past an electricity pylon and across to the start of the third peak **(Wp.9)**.

Our trail leads up in a steady climb to the small plateau at 368 metres altitude **(Wp.10, 35M)** - now that is what we call a panoramic view! We return by retracing our outward route to the tarmac road, and then the choice of descents into the resort.

Link to the TS-11 route to Adeje or Arona

Once on the third peak, we are close to the TS-11 **Arona-Adeje** walking route. To link to the TS-11, continue along the ridge north-east (**NE**) to its end, again taking care with footwork. We then descend on its western side in an easy scramble to relatively flat ground **(Wp.11)**. A faint trail with the remains of a stone wall on our right, pushes through the undergrowth to bring us to an abandoned cottage **(Wp.13)**. Beyond the cottage, a broad trail brings us onto the dirt *pista* of the TS-11 **(Wp.14)**.

7. DOWN TO TOWN

The TS-11 is one of the old donkey trail routes which links **Arona** and **Adeje** although the old route has unfortunately been disrupted by high level developments in **Torviscas Alto**. For the eastern arm, we have an easy country walk with impressive views, followed by the **Picos Las Américas** route for our descent into the resort, or in wet or windy weather walk down through the new developments to finish in **Torviscas**. Start with a relaxed ascent to **Arona** on the 480 Titsa bus service.

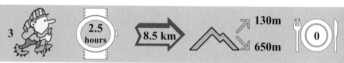

3   2.5 hours   8.5 km   130m / 650m   0

We start from the **Arona** bus terminus (**Wp.1, 0M**) by strolling up the **Calle Duque de la Torre** paved street to the town square (**Wp.2**) and go left across the square to walk up the top road to cross the TF-51 onto the **Vento** road (**Wp.3, 8M**). Walking up the **Vento** road, we pass **Casa del Pintur** on our right before our route runs down to the Obelisk junction (**Wp.4**) in **Vento**. Going left we pass the **Roque del Conde** path (**Wp.5, 18M**) just before going left on a *camino rural* tarmaced road.

The narrow road drops down through abandoned terraces, passing an impressive house (**Wp.6**), before coming down to a junction where another *camino rural* goes right across the *barranco* (**Wp.7**). After a short uphill houses line the road and we drop steeply down to the TF-51 main road (**Wp.8**). Watching out for traffic, we turn right to walk down the road past the 3km marker to an old loop of the road (**Wp.9**) and on to the start of **Camino Viejo de Adeje** (**Wp.10, 38M**) dirt road.

Beside the water channel on the TS-11, prickly pear (left), kleinia nerifolia and euphorbia canariensis (right).

On the dirt road, we sweep down to cross the watercourse of the first *barranco* (**Wp.11**). We climb up to pass an abandoned house on our left (**Wp.12**) before the cobbled trail zigzags down to cross the **Barranco del Rey** (**Wp.13**). A steady climb brings us up to meet the friendly dogs of a neat-walled farm (**Wp.14, 53M**). Passing the farm on our left, we stroll across the gentle slopes towards a low ridge which ends in a rocky outcrop. Passing a T-junction (**Wp.15**) where a dirt road goes right towards a white cottage, we continue ahead on the water-eroded trail which improves as we stroll up to meet a water channel on the ridge (**Wp.16, 60M**) from where we have spectacular views down over a *caldera* to **Los Cristianos** and **Playa de las Américas**.

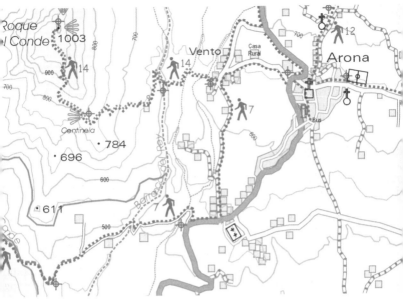

This ridge may seem fairly insignificant when seen from the east, but we face a steep descent on its west side. We zigzag down a donkey trail, its loose stone surface making for a slow, skittery descent until we cross a large working water canal (**Wp.17, 69M**) known locally as the **Río Conde**. Now we are on a gentle dirt path which runs alongside the **Río Conde** to give us an easy stroll along to a dirt road junction (**Wp.18),** where we turn downhill to a second junction (**Wp.19**). The main dirt road runs down to the water treatment works on the floor of the *caldera*, while we go right on a fainter trail onto a saddle (**Wp.20**) between a water change point on the canal, and the **Picos las Américas** on our left (**85M**).

Infrastructure and development have cut the traditional TS11 route, and we have three alternatives:

A

Picos Las Américas Route
Go left (**S**) past the abandoned cottage to climb up onto the third peak of **Picos las Américas**, and follow this route across the exposed ridges (do not attempt in windy or wet weather) to the road system above **San Eugenio Alto (30-40M)**, from where you have a choice of routes into the resort areas.

B
Go down into the development, and follow the roads down to the entrance of **Balcones del Conde (15-20M)**. Note that the road entrance may be closed at weekends below the current development works (November 2002).

C
Go up to the **Río Conde**, easiest from the first dirt road junction (**Wp.18**) and follow the canal above the development to meet our '**Adeje Skywalker**' route. We then have options to descend to the **Fañabe** area or to continue on the **Adeje Skywalker** route to **Adeje**.

8. ADEJE SKYWALKER

This is a spectacular new route with awesome views at almost every turn, but it comes at a price. While most of the route involves easy walking on a paved water canal, the **Río Conde**, we have to cross an extremely vertiginous aqueduct and edge around a mountain above sheer drops; a good head for heights and sure-footedness are essential. We named this route, 'Adeje Skywalker' for its elevated views over the south of Tenerife with the impression of being suspended above these southern landscapes.

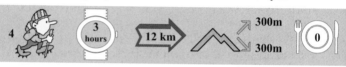

We start out from the bus stop by the **Adeje** *cementario* (cemetery), and in a few steps we go right onto a dirt road **(Wp.1),** passing an archaeological sign. Our dirt road winds down into the *barranco* to cross the water course **(Wp.2)** and come to a dirt cross roads.

We go over at the cross-roads to walk up the higher dirt road, passing through a metal gate **(Wp.3)** as we climb up onto the ridge at a U-bend **(Wp.4, 12M)**. Now the dirt road heads up the line of the ridge, passing a white cottage on our right and coming up to a junction just past a water tank **(Wp.5, 333m alt, 20M)**. Water pipes cross our route as we continue straight ahead on the dirt road towards the mountains. The road becomes rougher as we climb towards the mountains, passing *Naturaleza* signs **(Wp.6, 364m alt)** until we come to a faint path marked by a cairn **(Wp.7, 398m alt, 30M)** where the rough dirt road swings west **(W)**.

Taking the narrow path, we continue our steady ascent **(NE)** through the shrub-covered slopes, passing a small cairn **(Wp.8),** our path becoming

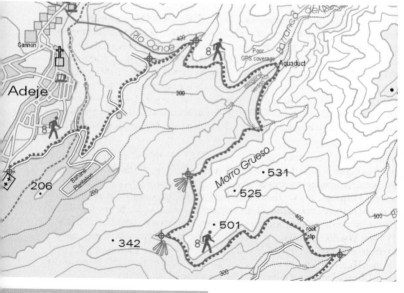

fainter as we gradually close with the canal. Finally we clamber up onto the canal (**Wp.9, 422m alt**) for a relaxing break after the long ascent of slogging up dirt roads and narrow paths.

We are on a broad (approximately 1m wide) paved water canal which gives us an elevated walkway with sensational views - surprisingly, unknown to other walking writers. This is an easy walking surface, but take care to 'look where you walk, and STOP to look at the views', as there is no protection from the drops alongside the canal. An easy stroll takes us over a small bridge (**Wp.10**) before curving round into a smaller *barranco* to cross its water course on another bridge (**Wp.11, 50M**), and walking out to a viewpoint (**Wp.12**).

As the canal turns into the next *barranco* it becomes vertiginous, with sheer drops on our right and a cliff on our left causing poor GPS coverage. If you have any doubts over this section, return towards **Adeje**.

We walk up to the major obstacle on our route, an aqueduct (**Wp.13**) carrying the canal over the steep **Barranco del Agua**, which drops down from **Roque Abinque.** In this dramatic orogenic setting of soaring mountains, cliffs and sheer *barrancos*, we edge over the twenty metre span, to a well-deserved rest at its eastern end (**60M**). After recovering from the aqueduct crossing, we soon face another vertiginous section where the canal runs under a cliff and there are some missing slabs; here we step onto the black water pipe to carefully negotiate these sections.

Turning out of the main **Barranco del Agua** ravine, we cross a small bridge (**Wp.14**) to enter a landscape of gentler slopes. After another bridge (**Wp.15**) we walk out to a *mirador* view (**Wp.16, 78M**) as the **Río Conde** swings left. A steel water pipe crosses the canal (**Wp.17**), just before we cross the **Morro Grueso** ridge (**Wp.18**) to swing above the **Fañabe** valley. We curve left (**Wp.19**) to see the **Río Conde** sweeping around the broad valley ahead of us.

Easy strolling takes us past a small cave (**Wp.20, 95M**) and over a small bridge (**Wp.21**), before we come to a section where rocks and earth cover the canal (**Wp.22**). Picking our way over the rock, we come back onto the paved canal to pass a dirt road on our right (**Wp.23**) and cross a small bridge (**Wp.24**) before coming to a water change point (**Wp.25, 110M**) where we drop down onto a dirt road which runs alongside the canal. We follow the dirt road until it swings right to drop into the valley (**Wp.26**) where we clamber back onto the paved canal. After crossing a bridge and a small canal which crosses the **Río Conde**, we come to a difficult water change point (**Wp.27**).

Some nimble footwork is needed to negotiate the inland scrub and change point to get back onto the paved canal. As we stroll on, the dirt road alongside the canal turns away towards an abandoned cottage on the saddle between two valleys (**Wp.28**), and we then climb over a small rock slip (**Wp.29**) and take care where there are occasional missing slabs, before we are below the 'White House' which sits above water change points which are numbered 195-9 and 194-8 (**Wp.30, 124M**). A couple of minutes later, the canal passes underground and is crossed by means of the rough dirt access road to the 'White House' (**Wp.31**) which gives us the choice of an uphill diversion to one of the region's most noticeable but least visited landmarks.

On the Río Conde, high above the southern coast.

Now we leave the **Río Conde** to head down the rough dirt road past a large water tank (**Wp.32**) on our left, to a junction of dirt roads (**Wp.33, 140M**), signed TS11 on our right. The dirt road is littered with shale and scree, making for slow skittery progress down past water tanks, those to the left (**Wp.34**) old and empty, and new and fenced to the right (**Wp.35**), before the dirt road heads straight down the side of the valley. Our walking surface improves as we pass dirt roads, to the left (**Wp.36**) and on the right (**Wp.37**), before we reach the first house and a tarmac lane (**Wp.38, 165M**). As we stroll down, we pass the impressive entrance to **Finca Amapola de Fañabe** (**Wp.39**) and then come onto the new road system behind the **Humbolt School** (**Wp.40, 170M**).

From here we can head past the school (**W**) on our left, to reach the access road alongside the motorway, or alternatively turn south (**S**) to follow the new roads towards the centre of the resort. (See the street plans in 'A Drive! Tenerife Touring Map for possible finish routes into the resort area.)

Alternative Finishes

Alternative finishes involve continuing on the **Río Conde** to the new developments and then heading down to **Torviscas Alto** on the new road system, or continuing past the new developments to join up with the eastern arm of the TS-11 to follow the **Picos Las Américas** route down into the resort.

9. TAUCHO TOUR

A circular walk with a surprise finish - sounds improbable, but for Taucho Tour it's true. This is an easy route on old donkey trails taking in spectacular views, excellent flora including an unusual floral phenomenon, and after a rather unpromising start the landscape exudes a bucolic charm; in short idyllic walking country, and with a classic *tipico* (**Bar Taucho**) not far away.

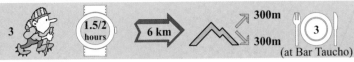

3 | 1.5/2 hours | 6 km | 300m / 300m | 3 (at Bar Taucho)

We start by driving west on the TF1 motorway and continue past the **Adeje** roundabout onto the TF82 and look for a right turning (easily missed) onto the TF583 road to **Taucho**. After the twisting, 3rd gear, ascent follow the narrow road through the village past the bus terminus (and **Bar Taucho**) and continue on the *camino rural* until you come to the church on your left and a parking area. Despite the bus terminus, TITSA's timetable does not include any services to the village!

From the corner of the church square (**Wp.1, 0M**) we stroll along **Calle La Serrería** before leaving it to go right (**Wp.2**) onto a smaller *camino rural*. Down into a small valley, the tarmac goes left to houses as we step right onto a broad dirt road (**Wp.3**) to continue (**S**) past large steel gates (**Wp.4**). Just after the gates a dirt *pista* goes left while we stay on the main dirt road which runs along to swing into a floriferous valley with a walking trail crossing the valley below us. We cross the valley's water course (**Wp.5**) to come gently uphill and meet the walking trail just before some steel gates.

Going left (**Wp.6**), we clamber up over rock to come onto the donkey trail's continuation as it skirts a fenced area, passing gates and an *embalse* (**Wp.7**), to come onto another dirt road. Soon we take a walking trail off to the right (**Wp.8**) alongside a small *barranco*, which soon curves right to cross the *barranco* floor (**Wp.9**) and then we come onto a dirt road arriving from the left (**Wp.10**). We swing along to a *parapente* launch point (**Wp.11**), with a most unusual official sign, to continue on a walking trail dropping into a steeper *barranco*. Across the watercourse (**Wp.12**), we climb up the southern wall, crossing a side *barranco* (**Wp.13**) for a final ascent to **Lomo de las Lajas** (**Wp.14, 28M**) with its impressive views over **Adeje** and the coast.

Leaving **Lomo de las Lajas**, we go east (**E**) to pick up the eroded walking trail (our 'Queen Of The South' route, and if you want really spectacular views go right to the top of the small ridge but take care) which climbs steadily and curves left for us to come up to a gentle open ridge (**Wp.15**) ahead of us.

A path takes us up the left side of the ridge ('Queen Of The South' route is a few metres to our right) in a steady climb, crossing a rock section (**Wp.16**) before coming onto the 'Queen Of The South' route. Continuing the steady climb, we come amongst the pines on a well defined path to reach a junction (**Wp.17, 47M**). Going left, we pass a large green dot to climb up to an **Ifonche** route sign on the crest of the ridge (**Wp.18**) with its carved water channels.

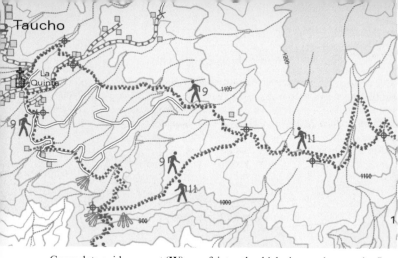

Green dots guide us west (**W**) on a faint path which zigzags down to the floor of the small valley (**Wp.19**), with an old cottage above us on our right, and then gently climbs up to cross a small ridge where we meet a steel water pipe (**Wp.20**). Now our path follows the water pipe steeply down into this unusual *barranco*. The *barranco* floor is completely choked with brambles which stretch as far as we can see in a great green phalanx we have not seen anywhere else. We zigzag down before following the southern side to cross the watercourse (**Wp.21, 58M**), at a cutting through the brambles, before climbing up over an old water canal to ascend the northern side still accompanied by the water pipe. As we climb to move away from the valley the bramble-choked watercourse is even more impressive until we turn away (**Wp.22**) to drop into another valley to cross its watercourse just below a mature pine (**Wp.23**), before a steady climb up for our path to cross open ground (**Wp.24**).

Houses are ahead of us as we descend alongside the pipe into another small valley (**Wp.25**) and climb up the path to cross open ground and into a minor valley (**Wp.26**) before climbing up the rough stone trail between stone walls to reach a *camino rural* (**Wp.27**) opposite a pair of houses. From here you can shortcut down the *camino rural* to the church, but we will go for a surprise finish.

Across the *camino rural* the water pipe continues past the fence of house Nº21, with its noisy dog. At first this looks an unlikely route but as we drop down the donkey trail emerges for us to descend steeply down its boulder-laid surface into the **Barranco de la Quinta**. Zigzags bring us steeply down, taking care on the slippery pine needles by a mature pine (**Wp.28**), to come onto the valley floor (**Wp.29**) at the bottom of the sheer-sided *barranco*. Green dots indicate a narrow path down the *barranco* floor, the rough boulders giving way to an easier surface before we emerge onto tarmac between **Taucho** and **La Quinta** (**Wp.30**). Ignoring a green arrow, we go left on the tarmac for a few metres to the start of a stone-laid trail (**Wp.31**) with a wooden handrail. The trail starts steeply and gets steeper as it zigzags up the *barranco* wall; far too steep for a safe descent. Puffing and panting, we come up to the back of a white cottage for the final climb up onto a dirt road where our start point is a few metres away on our right (**93M**) - now isn't that better than an easy finish!

10. WOW! SPECTACULAR

Just occasionally a walking route comes to light which has everything; spectacular views, awesome scenery, magnificent flora. Wow! Spectacular is just such a route, and has been missed by all other walking writers. If you only had time for one Tenerife walk, and are sure-footed with a head for heights, this is the route you should choose.

Do not attempt this route in wet or windy weather.

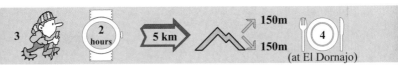

3   2 hours   5 km   150m / 150m   4 (at El Dornajo)

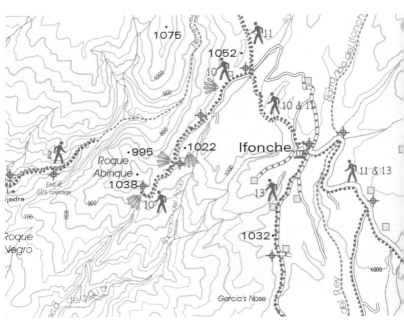

We start alongside **El Dornajo** in **Ifonche (Wp.1, 0M)**, to stroll down the tarmac lane (**W**) and turn right (**Wp.2**) onto a dirt road and then onto a *sendero* at a sign board (**Wp.3**). The path is way marked with green (new) and white (old) dots as we wind through two small valleys (**Wp.4**) amongst the pine-dotted slopes. Over a red earth spur, our trail drops down to cross a dirt road (**Wp.5, 12M**). Turning left, we stroll up the dirt road to pass a restored cottage (**Wp.6**) and come up to a large threshing circle on the lip of the *barranco* (**Wp.7**) with stunning views. We continue along the dirt road until it swings left (**Wp.8**) and then walk up to the remains of a sign board and a 'pa' sign (**Wp.9, 20M**).

The temptation is to continue up the broad ridge for the views from its head, but hidden beside the "pa" sign we take a stone-laid donkey trail which drops into the *barranco*. This amazing path winds down through a gateway (**Wp.10**) into a pocket of stunning flora; pruning shears are useful to keep the narrow path open through the vigorous vegetation. Our narrow path levels out to run beneath the outcrop's sheer cliffs, with the *barranco* plummeting down on our right, and careful footwork is needed on the narrower sections. From beneath the cliffs our path climbs up to bring us onto a saddle of sand-gold rock between the outcrop and **Roque Abinque**; more stunning views (**Wp.11, 35M**).

On the east of the saddle a small path, marked by cairns, runs along above the **Barranco del Agua**. Ahead **Playa de las Américas** is framed by the *barranco* walls, and a rock 'finger' indicates our destination. If you continue on the main path at a path junction (**Wp.12**), it will take you up to a stone corral perched on the ridge between the *barrancos*. We take the lower path which swings right above a water canal (**Wp.13**) and then crosses the canal (**Wp.14, 42M**) just before an eroded section (**Wp.15**) where we need to edge along the canal.

Our narrow path brings us onto the saddle by the rock 'finger' outcrop (**Wp.16**) before we go down to the right for stunning views from a ledge in the *barranco* wall (**Wp.17, 50M**) where a section of canal makes a comfortable seat in this most orogenic of landscapes. Take a picnic break on this mountain ledge drinking in one of Tenerife's most spectacular views.

Our route has been on an old, and largely forgotten, donkey trail which runs down to **Adeje**, but just beyond our finish point serious erosion starts and the trail is officially regarded as 'muy abandonado' which is unfortunate as, potentially, it would have been one of Tenerife's most stunning descents. We return by the same route.

Wow! Spectacular

11. QUEEN OF THE SOUTH

This walk certainly lives up to its 'royal' title. We start at the **Ifonche** junction and set out on a journey through a 'timescape' of agricultural settlements, pine forests, incredible *barrancos* and valleys, to emerge at the best *mirador* view in the south. The final descent of 650 metres altitude into **Adeje** is unfortunately more memorable for the rough track than the views - good footwear is essential - but don't let this put you off this grand walk.

To reach our start point we take the bus (N°s 342, 482) up to the **Ifonche** junction on the outskirts of **La Escalona** and walk up the road before dropping down to cross the **Barranco de Funes**. A stiff climb then brings us up onto the **Ifonche** plateau, followed by gentle strolling along the road passing two bars, the tiny church and the **El Refugio** turning, before going down into the **Barranco del Rey**. A further stiff climb then brings us up to the T-juntion at **Bar El Dornajo** (unlikely to be open before 13.00) in **Ifonche** (**Wp.1, 60M**).

An alternative, but much tougher, start can be made from **Arona** by walking up the **Vilaflor** road to the **Granja Arona** where we take the dirt road down to the *embalse* featured in our 'Fantasia' route. From the *embalse* you can take either the 'Fantasia' return route to **Ifonche** (**90M**) or the reverse of 'Fantasia' downward route, much more scenic but tougher and longer (**120M**).

At **Bar El Dornajo** (**Wp.1, 0M**) our 'Fantasia' route turns left, but today we follow the start of 'Wow! Spectacular' route (**Wps.2, 3 & 4**), until we come down to the dirt road in the bottom of the valley (**Wp.5, 12M**) where we head straight across the dirt road.

Our narrow walking trail climbs up from the valley floor and turns inland to steadily ascend the ridge. A steady ascent on the rough path brings us up to a bowl where terraces have been built amongst the pines, or perhaps where pines have colonised former agricultural terraces. We come to the end of a terrace wall, the trail continuing below the wall and climbing gently to bring us to the edge of the pine forest (**Wp.6, 17M**).

A clear trail leads into the forest, signed by a white arrow on a boulder, going gently uphill beneath the trees. We come up to a junction where we take the narrower needle-covered trail, following a white arrow, to climb steeply up towards the top of the ridge on our left. There are plenty of white arrow way marks to keep us on the path as we climb through a series of bends (**Wp.7**) to the crest of the ridge. On the ridge, large arrows made of rocks point in both directions along the path. A small cairn marks the continuation of the path and we go gently downhill. On our left we look down into the canyon of **Barranco del Infierno** and catch glimpses of the sea through the pines. Our trail runs downhill, with occasional climbs, along the wall of this magnificent canyon 250 metres above the route of our 'Barranco del Infierno' walk.

We walk below sheer cliffs, the long drop into the canyon on our left as we progress towards the head of the *barranco*. The path drops steeply, and we need to take care not to slip on the pine needle-covered trail, before levelling out to run below an impressive promontory. Sounds of running water and the waterfall come up from the canyon's depths, and passing through a rock channel, we go downhill to round a pocket in the canyon wall. The path runs down out of the pocket to round a promontory by a mature Canarian pine; from here we enjoy *mirador* views down into the sheer-sided *barranco*.

After the viewing point we come to a junction of paths (**Wp.8, 28M**). We take the right hand path, signed **TS3**, to climb steeply up the narrow trail along the *barranco* wall. The path zigzags up to come under cliffs as we continue through a rock channel, and then more cliffs before the ascent eases. We now stroll along to an area where the tumbled boulders of a huge rock slide cover the steep slopes. Our trail cuts through the sea of boulders to drop steeply down until we come out onto the floor of the canyon (**Wp.9, 38M**), now above the **Barranco del Infierno** and technically on the floor of **Barranco de la Fuente**.

Picking our way over the grey boulders, we come back onto the continuation of our route and start climbing up the western wall of the canyon.

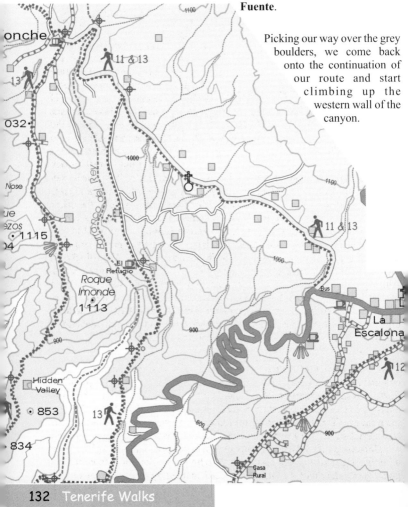

It's a stiff ascent on the steep rocky trail, which becomes covered in pine needles as we climb before the path levels out and we come under a large boulder. Our route undulates along the *barranco* wall before taking another climb. Pacing ourselves for the stiff ascent, and taking rests when necessary, we toil up to come above the canyon. Looking back across the *barranco* we can see that we have climbed back up to a similar altitude to the trail's start at **Ifonche**.

After the exertions of climbing out of the **Barranco de la Fuente** we might hope for some gentle downhill walking. However, the trail leaves the views behind and takes us into a rather sombre section of pine forest which clothes a land of valleys and sharp-sided *barrancos*. Our trail is clearly way marked with white dots and arrows, as we cross gentle valleys (**Wp.11**) and two sharp-sided *barrancos* (**Wps.12 & 13**) beneath the shade of the silent forest. A few cistus 'rock rose' bushes relieve the tedium of this brown needle-covered ground. As the valleys become shallower we need to pay careful attention to the route's way marking. Coming up a gentle slope we approach a pair of pines where the main path turns right (**Wp.14, 56M**); looking to our right we can see an arrow twenty metres up the gentle slope. Although this appears as a major junction both paths have the same destination, the right hand path crossing **Barranco Chavon** at **Wp.15** while the straight-on path crosses the steep **Barranco Chavon** at **Wp.16** and after climbing out of the *barranco*, runs on through the pines to a multi-junction of paths (**Wp.17, 72M**) where we join the upper crossing route.

From the rejoining of the trails the forest steadily changes, becoming more colourful as the trail leads us through a series of shallow valleys (**Wps.18, 19 & 20**) to come to a junction (**Wp.21, 88M**) at the edge of the forest. Ahead the main trail leads up onto an area of clear rock with a signboard (**Wp.22**), the main route to **Taucho**. Following the left hand trail we come onto bare rock to find a hand-carved rock water channel. Boots have worn faint trails across the rock for us to parallel the small water channel. Away on our right we look over a *barranco* to the outlying houses of **Taucho** village, as our path continues going gently downhill to an area of red earth marked by a cairn. If you go over

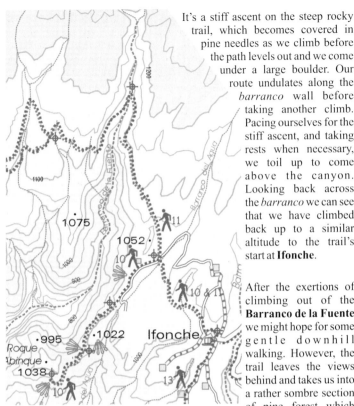

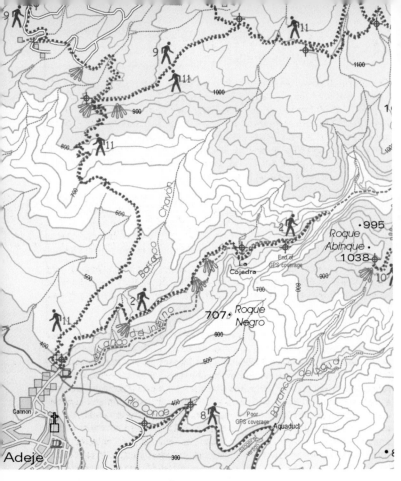

to your left at this point you will find the water channel again, and a spectacular view down over **Adeje** from the edge of the *cumbre*. This path swings right to run along below a low ridge and becomes very water-eroded before it meets a path (**Wp.23**) and then swings left onto the donkey trail at **Lomo de las Lajas (Wp.24, 107M)** with its superb panoramic views.

The descent from **Lomo de las Lajas** starts well on a stone-laid donkey trail descending below orange cliffs. However, at the end of this short section the trail deteriorates into a rocky, boulder strewn, path which has suffered from water erosion. For an alternative finish in **Taucho** see our 'Taucho Tour' route. It's a long, tortuous, winding route down the mountainside requiring continuous concentration on what must be the roughest trail on the island - well cushioned footwear is absolutely essential. Having to concentrate on every footfall doesn't allow much opportunity to look at the scenery, and makes the last hour of the walk seem even longer. Eventually the downward toil finishes when we meet the tarmac (**Wp.25**) and stroll down the smooth surface to the start of the **Barranco del Infierno** walk (**Wp.26, 197M**) at **Otello's** restaurant, although if it is Tuesday you will need to continue down into **Adeje** for refreshment, and buses back to the resorts.

12. WALKERS WHO LUNCH

Our downhill power walk descends from 1,050 metres altitude by a little-known route through rural countryside, taking in the county town of **Arona**. Finishing at 400 metres altitude in **Valle San Lorenzo** after descending through the impressive views seen at the start in **La Escalona**. We make no apologies for this walk being mostly on smooth tarmac, nor that it is all downhill and finishes at one of Tenerife's famous restaurants (but not expensive!) - the marvellous panoramic views and flora, plus an unusual garden fully justify this as a walking route.

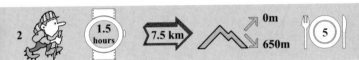

This walk is best saved for a relaxing day after you have completed all other routes. Take a gentle, scenic bus ride up to La Escalona (342 **Mount Teide** bus or 482 **Vilaflor** bus) and enjoy our downhill route finishing with a 'Power Lunch'.

In **La Escalona** the main road turns sharp left around the church square, and three other roads form a junction with the main road. Select the smallest road beside **Bar La Curva (Wp.1, 0M)**; the **San Miguel TF-565** road is on our the left. Leaving the junction, we follow the tiny road past a *correos* post box and round to the right past a small *ermita* to overlook our downhill route. Below us a vista of mountain slopes and peaks roll away to the coastal plain. The road, once the main donkey trail down to the county town of **Arona**, pays lip service to vehicles with a thin covering of tarmac, but few drivers know of or use this unmapped road. It is all downhill as the road drops steeply between farms, some working, others abandoned, and modern villas. Tarmac tracks lead off our narrow tarmac route, and terraces line both sides of the route, citrus groves and vines alternating with wild cacti, aloes, yuccas and endemic species.

Over on our right mounts **Conde** and **Imonde** dominate the landscape as we look down on the main road climbing up the valley. Downhill through this bucolic landscape we pass old and new houses, this little route is becoming a popular place to build your large villa in the country, including the *Casa Rural* **Correa del Almendro (Wp.2)**, until we come to where the *camino rural* swings sharp left **(Wp.3)**. Ahead, we go down a section of the old stone-laid donkey trail, passing an old farmhouse before rejoining the tarmac **(Wp.4)**. A few metres on we come to a cross and thoughtfully placed bench seat **(Wp.5)** if you would like a relaxed break at this point. The road continues steeply down, becomes **Calle San Antonio** and literally drops us down into the town square of **Arona (Wp.6, 38M)**.

On this first section we have descended 400 metres at an average slope of one in ten - a very good reason for choosing to walk the route downhill. At **Arona** there are bars off the town square for refreshment. Should you choose to finish walking here and return to the resort, continue straight over the town square down to the bus terminus and the 480 bus will take you to **Los Cristianos**.

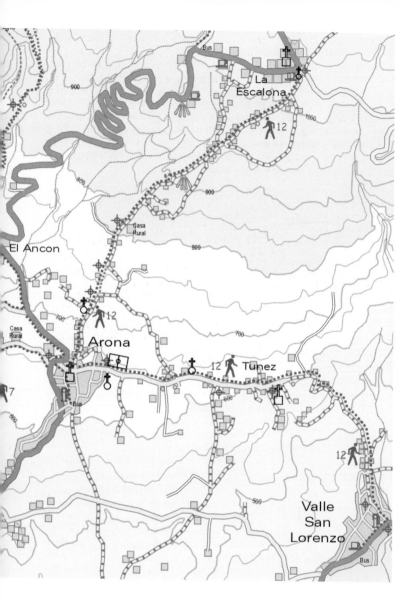

The second stage of our walk takes us out of **Arona** on the **Túnez** road (turn left at the end of **Calle San Antonio**) past the **RACE** office. In contrast to our steep descent into **Arona,** the **Túnez** road undulates around the 600 metre contour, even going uphill to pass the football stadium (**L**) and chapel (**R**) (**Wp.7**), before running along between a variety of homes ranging from simple habitations to Fort Knox style villas. One view not to be missed is after we pass a *camino rural* off to our right (**Wp.8**) an unusual garden starts on our right, modern sculptures and stonework mixing with a Japanese style in a most pleasing aspect. Passing the top of the property - note the hatchet and block - we find this most impressive of gardens is simply named number 66.

The next house, **La Esperanza**, was also briefly famous in the News of the World but is now better known for the large blue thing in its garden. Strolling on we pass **Túnez** church on our right (**Wp.9**) and head out into the country. Our road has narrowed, and when it swings right by a house and crosses a water canal, we start dropping down into the valley behind **Valle San Lorenzo**. Gentle strolling, with a few skittery steep sections, bring us down to the houses of the town and a Y-junction (**Wp.10**) where we go left. Down the narrow street we swing left and right to drop onto the main road (**Wp.11**) and go right. **Valle San Lorenzo** is in a state of parking gridlock, much easier to walk in and bus out, as we struggle (**SW**) past the petrol station to arrive at our destination (**Wp.12, 87M**); **Cafeteria Paraíso**.

Behind the simple exterior is one of the most popular eating places in the south of Tenerife with an extensive menu, good service and good prices (reservations essential in the evenings). One skinflint expat. describes this establishment as expensive, but all thinking people will recognise the top quality and excellent value that makes it so popular, though this may mean that we have to wait for a table. As a walker you will empathise with the understated sporting excellence of **Cafeteria Paraíso**; the *parapente* pilots you may have seen landing on the town outskirts are regulars here. Head honcho, Alejandro, is a well respected triathalon competitor (his younger brother is a professional footballer), Clara is a former Gran Canaria triathalon champion, and Toño (the owner) is famous for his Fiat-Abarth car racing; if you have some free time, ask him about his cars! Also the 416 bus stop is just outside for the service down to **Los Cristianos**.

13. FANTASIA

We make no apologies for borrowing the famous Disney film title to describe this spectacular walk. Our route takes us from scene to scene, almost as if the landscape is being transformed around us. Whether it is the mountains, spectacular views, hidden valley, verdant plant life, or the unusual geology which you find most breathtaking, the sum of all these parts is pure 'Fantasia' - truly one of the south's most spectacular walks. Designed as a circular walk for car drivers, this route can be made linear to **Arona** or **Vento** if you are using the TITSA bus service; reduce exertion rating to 3 walker.

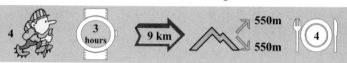

4 | 3 hours | 9 km | 550m / 550m | 4

Start for bus users
We start by catching the 342 or 482 bus up to the **Ifonche** junction (**Cruce de Ifonche**) bus stop. From the junction we walk up the steep start of the **Ifonche** road to swing across the **Barranco de Funes** and climb up to the **Ifonche Plateau**. For the first hour we follow the quiet road down past **Bar Pedro** and passing the turning to **El Refugio** (**Wp.26**), before dropping into the **Barranco de Ifonche** (**Wp.28**) and a stiff climb up to **Bar El Dornajo** (**Wp.29, 3.2km**), usually open from 13.00, closed Thursdays) in **Ifonche**. If you can get a lift or taxi to **Ifonche** you can reduce the walking time by one hour.

At **El Dornajo** we turn left (**S**) to walk along the narrow road passing another tiny road going up to the left while we continue straight on. As we stroll down below a terrace wall, away on our right is an impressive farming settlement, its massive terrace walls giving the look of a fortified promontory. After running downhill, the road climbs quite steeply up to a house before levelling out to run along a ridge for us to come to a road junction with a sturdy wooden cross set in a concrete base (**Wp.1, 4km**) where a road drops down into the valley on our left.

Start for car users
Follow the same directions as for bus travellers and park near the wooden cross; often parking at **El Dornajo** is rather fraught.

Onward route
From the cross (**Wp.1, 0M**) we stroll along the ridge on the road heading towards **Roque Imonde**. On our right we pass a huge head-shaped rock outcrop, **Garcia's Nose**, as we come under the heights of **Roque de los Brezos**. Our route goes gently downhill through Canarian pines as we walk above large abandoned terraces below us on the left, undulating along below **Roque de los Brezos** to come above cultivated terraces and a farm house. Ahead is the saddle between **Roque Imonde** and **Roque de los Brezos** which is our first destination.

As the road swings left to run down to the farmhouse, look for a path (**Wp.2, 8M**) which runs below the ridge to cross the open ground and climb gently up to the saddle. If you miss the first path, look for a white marker post below the road on your right just before reaching the farmhouse. A faint trail goes down below a terrace and across to a derelict building, from which you go up over open ground to the saddle. Do not go past the farmhouse on the road as its backyard is filled with hunting dogs and a couple of guard dogs!

As we reach the saddle a spectacular view over the resort of **Playa de las Américas** welcomes our arrival. Set on the saddle is a large threshing circle (**Wp.3**) dating from the old days when the terraces stretching up the slopes of **Roque Imonde** were cultivated. From the threshing circle, we walk a few metres up the spine to find a narrow walking trail which runs around the west side of the mountain under a large rock outcrop with a green paint mark. We follow the rough trail as it traverses the steep slopes, wild plants abounding on these moist western slopes. Magnificent views are always with us on this section - remember to 'Stop to look, and look where you put your feet'. Our path runs into and out of pockets in the side of the mountain above the heads of *barrancos* down below us, undulating around promontories (**Wp.4** marks rounding the first promontory) and through pockets with an occasional steep descent. Parts of the trail suffer from water erosion and combined with the occasional loose rock surface, we carefully pick our way around the mountain.

A gentle climb as the path comes up to round a promontory on red rock, heralds a change in the nature of our route. We turn around lichen-covered rock into another pocket to pass small volcanic 'blow holes' in the rock on our left. Taking care crossing water-eroded sections of the path for two narrow sections of path (**Wp.5, 27M**), we climb out of the pocket onto a spur running down from **Roque Imonde**. **Roque del Conde** comes back into view as we reach the spur and we look down onto the gentle landscape of the **Hidden Valley** (**Wp.6**). Neat, though abandoned, terraces ring this bowl in the mountains where in spring field marigolds create a golden carpet, adding to the atmosphere. Our path runs down the promontory to turn down into the valley, the loose rock path zigzagging down the slope before running along a rock channel. Down over coloured rock, we cross an old water channel (**Wp.7**) and emerge above the valley's top terrace. Taking care not to get spiked by prickly pear, we come down to the threshing circle (**Wp.8, 40M**), set on the saddle between the rounded hills.

The **Hidden Valley** is an ideal place to take a break if you wish to explore the remains of this once self-sufficient pocket in the mountains. Several caves had been converted to agricultural use, and a stone-roofed water cistern provided a substantial water resource for the small community. You could easily spend an hour or two exploring this idyllic environment.

To leave the **Hidden Valley**, we walk up from the threshing circle in the direction of **Roque del Conde**. As we climb we come onto a faint trail which passes a pair of caves on our left as it circles a rounded ridge. After levelling out the path runs below the rounded peak on our left and above a sharp sided *barranco* on our right, before climbing gently to round the promontory. We come to a rock outcrop on our right with beautiful views across to the ridges of **Roque de los Brezos** and down over **Adeje**. Below us, our onward route snakes through an unusual geological formation of sharp ridges towards the **Degollada de los Frailitos**. From a gnarled outcrop of rock we swing left and

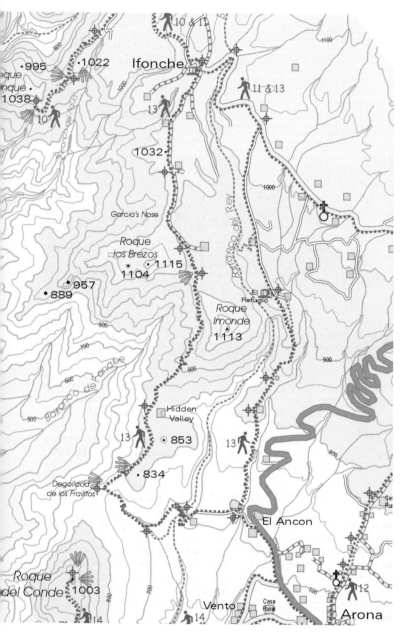

gradually drop down the gravely path between vertical plates of rock and onto the *degollada*.

We follow the faint trail towards the saddle of **Degollada de los Frailitos** to pass an outcrop of shattered rock (**Wp.9, 52M**) with views over **Adeje** to the west coast, while across from us an unusual natural rock arch tops the jagged ridge running down from **Roque de los Brezos**. Our trail runs out to the

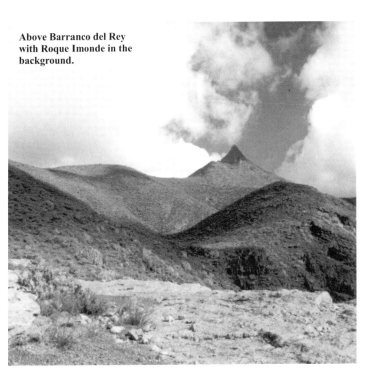

Above Barranco del Rey with Roque Imonde in the background.

degollada (**Wp.10**), where we turn our backs on **Adeje** and head down over rock slopes with ancient abandoned terraces on our right. Occasional stone cairns mark a faint trail down to strike a broken down rock wall at the edge of the terraces, where the path becomes clearer. Keeping the wall on our right, we follow its line until the path swings left across the rock slopes to cross a small watercourse. Our trail wanders along and then zigzags (**Wp.11, 59M**) down to cross the watercourse (**Wp.12**) again.

The narrow walking trail meanders along the right hand (**S**) side of the watercourse through a wild hillside below ancient terraces. Our clear but narrow trail comes down beside the watercourse to a faint junction (**Wp.13, 65M**), where we follow the main trail over the watercourse to climb around the hillside on a clear dirt path which brings us to the lip of the **Barranco del Rey** and along to the top of an old donkey trail dropping into the *barranco* (**Wp14, 70M**). It is a steep, zigzagging, descent requiring careful footwork before emerging on the floor of the *barranco* by a "pa" sign (**Wp.15, 74M**); just the place to take a cool break in the shade (mornings) before tackling the long ascent back to **Ifonche**.

A few metres down the *barranco* we come to the restart of the *sendero*. It is onwards and upwards on the boulder-laid trail to steadily climb up through a series of zigzags, taking rests when necessary. The path levels out at an area of red earth below small cliffs, giving us *mirador* views back over a landscape untouched by man for decades. From the red earth, the path runs along the lip of the *barranco* below the cliffs (**Wp.16**) before turning left to climb up over rock and away from the *barranco* on a rough path to come alongside abandoned terraces. The tiled roof of a cottage comes into view as our route follows the edge of the terraces to pass behind the cottage (**Wp.17**). From the cottage we follow a rough donkey trail up between tumbled stone walls, passing a disused water cistern on our right, to come onto a dirt road. It's a gentle stroll along the dirt road as it starts to run downhill to come below the wall of an *embalse* (**Wp.18, 86M**).

Linear walkers should continue on the main dirt road where a rock and concrete bridge crosses the **Barranco del Ancón**. From the bridge it is a steady climb up the rough dirt road to meet the main road at the **La Granja de Arona** restaurant (open from 13.00 - but closed Tuesdays) for a ten minute stroll down the main road (watch out for the traffic) to turn left by the **Centro de Acogida de Arona** and walk down **Calle Prolongación D'Alfonso** to **Arona** town square. Another alternative is to go right at the **Vento** junction, signed **Roque del Conde**, to pick up our **Arona** to **Playa las Américas** route.

For us circular walkers we now start to pay for all that downhill as we go up a rocked-off dirt road signed to **El Refugio**. Coming up round the *embalse* we face slopes of abandoned farm land stretching up to the horizon. A rough path, well waymarked with white splodges, takes us up between the picturesque **Barranco del Ancón** and a large water channel. It is a steady, relentless ascent, which distracts from the beautiful views, to cross a metal water pipe (**Wp.19**) before coming up to a tumbled cottage (**Wp.20, 108M**). After the cottage the gradient eases for us to stroll up to a circular water tank (**Wp.21**) and cross the water channel to walk across to abandoned terraces. Now the ascent starts again as the white splodged path takes us up through the old terraces onto a steep section of the path which brings a white house into view. Before reaching the house white splodges guide us off the path (**Wp.22**) to climb up onto a really rough old rock road. It is a stiff climb up to pass the white house and come onto a dirt road with the welcoming sight of **El Refugio** ahead; a final few metres bring us up to this unique hostelry (**Wp.23, 133M**).

Suitably refreshed we head up the dirt road to pass a goat farm (**L**), and dirt road (**R**) (**Wp.24**). For the adventurous you can descend into **Barranco del Rey** on a donkey trail behind the goat farm; unfortunately the continuation on the far slope has been long abandoned leading to a lively ascent. Our choice is to continue up the dirt road, passing a dirt road off to the right (**Wp.25**), to the **Ifonche** road (**Wp.26, 149M**) to turn left and follow the tarmac. As we drop into the **Barranco del Rey** there is an intriguing dirt road off to the left (**Wp.27**) before we come down to the watercourse (**Wp.28, 159M**) where a **Vilaflor** walking route is signed off the road. A steep climb brings us up to **El Dornajo** (**Wp.29**) for the possibility of more refreshment before heading out on the narrow tarmac lane to our starting point (**Wp.1, 174M**).

14. TABLE MOUNTAIN

Roque del Conde's 1000 metres 'table top' peak dominates the coastal plain of southern Tenerife. From the top, the views are simply stupendous, rewarding the stiff climb up this impressive mountain, which will also appeal to plant enthusiasts. This route is for fit walkers who can confidently tackle the climb totalling 450 metres on rough tracks requiring good, well cushioned, walking footwear.

4 | 3.5 hours | 11 km | 450m / 450m | 3 (in Arona)

Our starting point is at the junction of the **Vento** road with the TF-51, just above **Arona**'s town square, where there is plenty of parking; please do not park on the narrow roads in **Vento** village. If arriving by bus, then from the **Arona** terminus walk up the street to the town square to take the **Calle Prolongación D'Alfonso** from the north-west corner of the square. Climbing up the steep street we then cross carefully over the main road to our start point by the public telephone (**Wp.1, 0M**).

We climb up from the main road to views down to the coast as the lane swings left and past **La Casa del Pintur** *casa rural* (**Wp.2**) before the lane runs down between the first houses of **Vento**. We stroll down to the religious obelisk at the T-junction (**Wp.3, 6M**) and turning left we come down to the **Roque del Conde** path (**Wp.4**) signed off to our right by house number 78.

After the tarmac we are on a well-made *sendero* which drops us down into the **Barranco de las Casas (Wp.5)**. Our trail runs up over rock to a crest and then drops us down the **Barranco del Ancón (Wp.6)**. Across the valley floor, a gentle climb brings us up to walk alongside the *barranco*, passing a path off to our left (**Wp.7**), until our trail swings right across a water channel to a junction of paths. We go straight ahead over rock to a 'pa' sign (**Wp.8**) and confront the **Barranco del Rey**. At the lip of the *barranco* wall we come onto a well-made *sendero* which zigzags steeply down towards the *barranco* floor. Stone walls, with posts mounted in them, line the *sendero* as we drop down on its rough boulder surface. After twists and turns we come onto the valley floor (**Wp.9, 22M**) just above a waterfall (when water runs down the *barranco*) with sheer cliff walls rising fifty metres up on each side of us.

Straight across the valley floor, we come onto another rough boulder *sendero*, marked by white arrows, and start climbing. We toil up the stiff climb, which gets steeper as we get higher, until a set of stone steps brings us to the top of the *barranco* wall (**Wp.10**). Ahead, **Roque del Conde** looms over us as a prominent trail goes right but we take the path to the left. Climbing up past a white arrow, our dirt path winds it way up to a gold rock slab, with views back to **Vento**, and continues on towards a crumbling cottage.

Over a small crest the path runs down past a small water cistern (**Wp.11**) the size of a bath, on our right. Above the water cistern, unseen by most walkers, is an opening in the rock. Climbing up the rock slope we find ourselves looking through the narrow opening into a large subterranean cavern. A small

On the map labels: 834, Degollada de los Frailitos, El Ancon, difficult water-change point, 8, Roque del Conde 1003, 14, 700, 800, 900, 695, 700, 800, 600, Vento, 14, Casa Rural, 700, Bus, 7, Centinela, 784, 696, 600, Barranco del Rey, 611, 500, 7, Río Conde, 68

channel, now mostly silted up, guides water into the cavern. In the far distant past, long before pipes and water channels, this substantial cistern was the main water storage in this

One of the views from Roque del Conde - Playa de Las Américas far below.

area. You can get an idea of the cavern's size by shouting into it and waiting for the echo! Leaving this historical site we drop back down onto the path to continue on to the cottage (**Wp.12, 30M**).

Our trail climbs up past the north wall of the cottage. We pass two threshing circles on our left (**Wps.13 & 14**) as we continue up over the abandoned terraces to come onto a boulder-laid donkey trail (**Wp.15**) to continue straight uphill. Our trail swings left for us to head diagonally across the slope in a relentless climb towards the saddle at **Centinela**. At the end of the 'long straight', the donkey trail becomes rougher and continues upwards through a series of zigzags as we climb towards the saddle. It is a steep, relentless climb so pace yourself and take rests whenever necessary. We come onto another 'long straight' of the donkey trail and continue toiling upwards. Ahead large birds circle above the ridge, like buzzards in a western but here, only seagulls!

The donkey trail swings right for another 'long straight' pointing towards **Roque del Conde**, before swinging left for the last 'long straight' of the route.

At the end of the last 'long straight' we swing right and the donkey trail finishes for us to continue climbing on a narrow dirt path. We climb steeply up through a series of zigzags to reach the saddle at **Centinela (Wp.16, 51M)**. The path opens out into a small clear area, like an unofficial *mirador*. As we climb onto the ridge, spectacular views open up over the resort of **Playa de las Américas** over 700 metres below us.

We take a break on the *mirador* to enjoy the vistas laid out below us. East, our start point in **Arona**, can be seen 150 metres below our present position, and this difference in altitude leads us to question our next step. From the *mirador* it is a narrow, often rough, path which includes steep climbs totalling 250 metres to the top of **Roque del Conde**, and 250 metres back down to the *mirador*. If at this point you are very tired, then rest at the *mirador* before returning the same way down to **Vento** and **Arona**. Similarly, if you encounter bad weather, or if **Conde** has become cloud covered, finish at **Centinela** and return to **Arona**.

From **Centinela** a narrow path goes right (**NW**) along the ridge towards **Roque del Conde**, marked by white paint. Our route undulates along to take us across the southern face of the mountain until we swing right (**Wp.17**) for a zigzag ascent. We come above the hidden valley which lies behind **Playa de las Américas**, the head of the valley and one ridge filled with *embalses* while the floor is covered with banana plantations. The loose rock and dirt path climbs steeply to bring us up onto sheets of orange rock below ten metre high cliffs (**Wp.18**). Going left, we continue to circle the mountain following the trail as it climbs around rock promontories. It is onwards and upwards through a series of steep climbs, the path splitting (**Wp.19**) and rejoining (**Wp.20**) just above a 'TS4' white paint marker.

A final toiling ascent brings us onto the edge of the plateau (**Wp.21, 83M**), and a surprise. On the mountain-top we find long abandoned agricultural terraces - sometime in the distant past someone used to farm this least-accessible area of land! A path, trodden down by walkers, leads across the terraces towards the mound and height marker at the official peak of **Roque del Conde**. As we approach the peak we find the large mound covered in a sea of asphodels (Asphodelus tenuifolius), a beautiful sight when in flower February - May. Pushing through the flowers we come to the height marker (**Wp.22, 88M**). **Roque del Conde** is the final mountain in the chain surrounding **Las Cañadas**, and inland is the 'turret' peak of **Roque Imonde**. Here, standing suspended high above the surrounding lands, we have awesome views over the south and west coasts - a fitting reward for the effort of the climb.

We return by the same route; there is no other way up or down; taking extreme care on the steep descent down to the *mirador*. After the *mirador* the path and donkey trail make for an easier descent, though it can be hard on the knees. The climbs out of the three *barrancos*, particularly **Barranco del Rey**, give a small reminder of our earlier efforts before we arrive back at **Arona**.

GERANIUM WALK

Tenerife's longest sea-front promenade, 'Geranium Walk', stretches from the **Costamar** apartments at the south-eastern tip of **Los Cristianos** all the way through the resorts of **Los Cristianos**, **Playa las Americas**, **Playa Fañabe** and **Costa Adeje** to the developing village of **La Caleta**.

Originally named by us in our 1988 street plans, 'Geranium Walk' was soon adopted as the official name for this coastal promenade. Since 1988, development has extended westwards, increasing the length of the promenade from 7 kilometres to its present 9.8 kilometres.

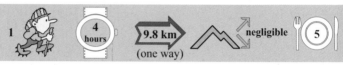

1   **4 hours**   **9.8 km** (one way)   negligible   5

Geranium Walk contrasts with our country and mountain routes, giving you an urban experience of southern Tenerife. Dress is strictly informal, footwear is comfortable casual, and speed is not of the essence. Bars and restaurants beyond count line the route, obviating the need for supplies, and navigation is as simple as it can be. Best maps are the Street Plans included in 'Tenerife Indestructible Map' and 'Drive Tenerife Touring Map', both of which have the latest street plans, and are the only maps to include **Playa Fañabe** and **Costa Adeje**.

Finding Geranium Walk is simplicity itself. Simply walk towards the sea until you come to the pedestrian walkway. Our preference is to start at **Costamar** and finish at **La Caleta**. Few directions are needed, but at the end of **Los Cristianos** beach as you come to the fresh fish stalls, go right to walk through the tunnel to emerge alongside **Playa las Vistas**. After the seaward side of the notorious **Veronicas**, go right and follow the pavement past **Playas Troya** up to the roundabout; the bar just below the walkway makes a suitable refreshment stop with views over the frolicking sunbathers. Just past the roundabout, Geranium Walk leaves the road to run down to **Playa Bobo** before the **Bouganville** stairs bring us back up onto the headland.

At **Puerto Colón** marina, take the stairs down to circle **Playa La Pinta** before rounding the headland to **Playa Fañabe**, with the impressive **Bahía del Duque** hotel ahead of us.

Past **Playa Fañabe**, the new hotels become even more impressive before finishing at the **Costa Adeje Palace** hotel, inland of which is the **Ermita de San Sebastián**. We walk down to a new beach which we cross on a slatted walkway before coming up to the **La Caleta** road. A short stroll takes us through the new developments of **La Caleta** before turning left down a pedestrian walkway, to emerge at the seafront bar for refreshments while contemplating the return stroll.

See the notes on GPS use and waypoints in the introduction on page 11.

1.

LIFE IN THE RAW

Wp	N	W
1	28 06.009	16 45.207
2	28 06.137	16 45.319
3	28 06.178	16 45.336
4	28 06.264	16 45.274
5	28 06.248	16 45.391
6	28 06.259	16 45.502
7	28 06.273	16 45.508
8	28 06.405	16 45.489
9	28 06.514	16 45.585
10	28 06.532	16 45.635
11	28 06.547	16 45.645
12	28 06.551	16 45.698
13	28 06.565	16 45.751
14	28 06.583	16 45.770
15	28 06.690	16 45.704
16	28 06.693	16 45.754
17	28 06.834	16 45.755
18	28 06.846	16 45.746
19	28 06.893	16 45.765
20	28 06.875	16 45.859
21	28 06.846	16 45.849
22	28 06.796	16 45.917
23	28 06.708	16 45.954
24	28 06.606	16 45.978
25	28 06.535	16 45.996
26	28 06.550	16 45.919
27	28 06.442	16 45.522
28	28 06.032	16 45.451
29	28 06.003	16 45.440
30	28 06.062	16 45.366

2.

BARRANCO DEL INFIERNO

Wp	N	W
1	28 07.491	16 43.316
2	28 07.630	16 43.107
3	28 07.722	16 43.053
4	28 07.648	16 43.032
5	28 07.735	16 42.883
6	28 07.818	16 42.749
7	28 07.735	16 42.696
8	28 07.906	16 42.676
9	28 07.917	16 42.617
10	28 07.902	16 42.532
11	28 07.945	16 42.433
12	28 07.945	16 42.405
13	28 07.958	16 42.354

3.

BARREN GRANDEUR

Wp	N	W
1	28 02.596	16 42.471
2	28 02.380	16 42.410
3	28 02.430	16 42.297
4	28 02.428	16 42.164
5	28 02.414	16 42.183
6	28 02.324	16 42.202
7	28 02.286	16 42.330
8	28 02.181	16 42.392
9	28 02.070	16 42.315
10	28 01.936	16 42.263
11	28 01.927	16 42.258
12	28 01.853	16 42.223
13	28 01.761	16 42.153
14	28 01.765	16 42.135
15	28 01.706	16 42.195
16	28 01.674	16 42.176
17	28 01.241	16 42.230
18	28 01.193	16 42.233
19	28 01.040	16 42.266
20	28 00.953	16 42.248
21	28 00.918	16 42.244
22	28 00.875	16 42.219
23	28 00.393	16 42.167
24	28 00.185	16 41.951
25	28 00.214	16 41.889
26	28 00.257	16 41.730
27	28 00.213	16 41.688
28	28 00.144	16 41.604
29	28 00.015	16 41.527
30	27 59.985	16 41.553
31	28 00.358	16 41.697
32	28 00.398	16 41.748
33	28 00.469	16 41.774
34	28 00.518	16 41.782
35	28 00.656	16 41.711
36	28 00.761	16 41.718
37	28 00.900	16 41.645
38	28 00.882	16 41.596
39	28 01.392	16 41.328
40	28 01.720	16 41.096
41	28 01.945	16 41.258
42	28 01.924	16 41.367
43	28 01.957	16 41.430
44	28 02.137	16 41.562
45	28 02.155	16 41.713
46	28 02.344	16 41.983
47	28 02.404	16 42.012

3.

ALTERNATIVE FINISH - BARREN GRANDEUR

Wp	N	W
1	28 00.005	16 41.525
2	27 59.869	16 41.160
3	27 59.855	16 40.813
4	27 59.885	16 40.538
5	27 00.044	16 40.456
6	27 00.184	16 40.356
7	27 00.255	16 39.917
8	27 00.320	16 39.949
9	27 00.342	16 39.919
10	28 00.450	16 39.632
11	28 00.332	16 39.107
12	28 00.535	16 39.076
13	28 00.613	16 38.703
14	28 00.576	16 38.367

4.

MOUNT GUAZA

Wp	N	W
1	28 02.514	16 42.251
2	28 02.435	16 42.299
3	28 02.429	16 42.170
4	28 02.465	16 42.096
5	28 02.450	16 42.059
6	28 02.436	16 42.044
7	28 02.403	16 42.011
8	28 02.380	16 41.960
9	28 02.328	16 41.861
10	28 02.314	16 41.828
11	28 02.460	16 41.724
12	28 02.517	16 41.673
13	28 02.552	16 41.586
14	28 02.844	16 41.338
15	28 02.892	16 41.315
16	28 02.994	16 41.343
17	28 02.063	16 41.576
18	28 02.940	16 41.633
19	28 02.895	16 41.651

5.

COASTAL ESCAPISM

Wp	N	W
1A	28 00.595	16 38.222

Wp	N	W
2A	28 00.684	16 38.055
3A	28 00.672	16 37.945
4A	28 00.663	16 37.907
5A	28 00.666	16 37.859
1	28 00.468	16 38.240
2	28 00.472	16 38.129
3	28 00.490	16 37.966
4	28 00.496	16 37.953
5	28 00.482	16 37.886
6	28 00.491	16 37.846
7	28 00.643	16 37.819
8	28 00.675	16 37.823
9	28 00.774	16 37.704
10	28 00.825	16 37.676
11	28 00.937	16 37.522
12	28 01.069	16 37.198
13	28 01.069	16 37.100
14	28 01.072	16 37.084
15	28 01.056	16 37.023
16	28 01.109	16 36.961
17	28 01.133	16 36.912
18	28 01.258	16 36.546
19	28 01.314	16 36.471
20	28 01.323	16 36.383
21	28 01.351	16 36.258
22	28 01.482	16 36.314
23	28 01.523	16 36.182
24	28 01.501	16 36.080
25	28 01.537	16 35.900
26	28 01.592	16 35.834
27	28 01.628	16 35.715
28	28 01.702	16 35.596

6.
PICOS LAS AMÉRICAS
(Town section)

Wp	N	W
1	28 04.536	16 43.728
2	28 04.552	16 43.648
3	28 04.542	16 43.612
4	28 04.540	16 43.510
5	28 04.549	16 43.452
6	28 04.542	16 43.377
7	28 04.558	16 43.329
8	28 04.621	16 43.234
9	28 04.590	16 43.216
10	28 04.813	16 43.132
11	28 04.904	16 43.116
12	28 04.925	16 43.113

(Picos section)

Wp	N	W
1	28 04.929	16 43.108
2	28 05.122	16 43.066
3	28 05.152	16 43.008
4	28 05.209	16 42.970
5	28 05.218	16 42.954
6	28 05.256	16 42.874
7	28 05.293	16 42.560
8	28 05.293	16 42.533
11	28 05.361	16 42.466
13	28 05.452	16 42.368
14	28 05.489	16 42.326

7.
DOWN TO TOWN

Wp	N	W
1	28 05.817	16 40.775
2	28 05.937	16 40.730
3	28 05.985	16 40.849
4	28 06.015	16 41.135
5	28 05.984	16 41.159
6	28 05.841	16 41.113
7	28 05.613	16 41.154
8	28 05.467	16 41.153
9	28 05.452	16 41.247
10	28 05.434	16 41.287
11	28 05.509	16 41.271
12	28 05.457	16 41.452
13	28 05.468	16 41.510
14	28 05.417	16 41.589
15	28 05.358	16 41.722
16	28 05.247	16 41.855
17	28 05.333	16 41.977
18	28 05.502	16 42.129
19	28 05.511	16 42.237
20	28 05.492	16 42.324

8.
ADEJE SKYWALKER

Wp	N	W
1	28 06.896	16 43.536
2	28 07.035	16 43.262
3	28 06.994	16 43.219
4	28 06.925	16 43.237
5	28 07.119	16 43.068
6	28 07.237	16 42.989
7	28 07.287	16 42.923
8	28 07.322	16 42.837
9	28 07.342	16 42.813
10	28 07.347	16 42.787
11	28 07.287	16 42.658
12	28 07.198	16 42.645
13	28 07.275	16 42.436
14	28 07.037	16 42.496
15	28 07.005	16 42.570
16	28 06.875	16 42.784
17	28 06.691	16 42.826
18	28 06.667	16 42.886
19	28 06.552	16 42.765
20	28 06.674	16 42.550
21	28 06.728	16 42.419
22	28 06.673	16 42.300
23	28 06.624	16 42.302
24	28 06.600	16 42.183
25	28 06.547	16 42.234
26	28 06.478	16 42.324
27	28 06.372	16 42.369
28	28 06.255	16 42.411
29	28 06.202	16 42.431
30	28 06.057	16 42.544
31	28 06.022	16 42.462
32	28 05.886	16 42.467
33	28 05.872	16 42.504
34	28 05.816	16 42.709
35	28 05.913	16 42.823
36	28 05.915	16 42.926
37	28 05.743	16 43.126
38	28 05.664	16 43.258
39	28 05.671	16 43.332
40	28 05.635	16 43.427

9.
TAUCHO TOUR

Wp	N	W
1	28 08.902	16 43.513
2	28 08.875	16 43.496
3	28 08.837	16 43.491
4	28 08.769	16 43.453
5	28 08.701	16 43.378
6	28 08.671	16 43.406
7	28 08.658	16 43.368
8	28 08.652	16 43.297
9	28 08.643	16 43.272
10	28 08.611	16 43.267
11	28 08.571	16 43.222
12	28 08.607	16 43.098
13	28 08.499	16 43.112
14	28 08.457	16 43.177
15	28 08.479	16 42.988
16	28 08.611	16 42.819
17	28 08.718	16 42.550
18	28 08.726	16 42.610
19	28 08.779	16 42.651
20	28 08.806	16 42.694
21	28 08.826	16 42.745
22	28 08.866	16 42.867
23	28 08.896	16 42.966
24	28 08.878	16 43.101
25	28 08.907	16 43.177
26	28 08.974	16 43.235
27	28 08.991	16 43.272
28	28 09.055	16 43.318
29	28 09.050	16 43.342
30	28 08.997	16 43.438
31	28 08.963	16 43.472

10.
WOW! SPECTACULAR

Wp	N	W
1	28 08.014	16 41.289
2	28 08.032	16 41.340
3	28 08.076	16 41.354
4	28 08.134	16 41.470
5	28 08.278	16 41.526
6	28 08.258	16 41.608
7	28 08.232	16 41.651
8	28 08.136	16 41.698
9	28 08.119	16 41.709
10	28 08.096	16 41.749
11	28 07.966	16 41.858
12	28 07.945	16 41.856
13	28 07.916	16 41.877
14	28 07.907	16 41.906
15	28 07.886	16 41.921
16	28 07.841	16 41.931
17	28 07.852	16 41.970
20	28 08.710	16 42.518
21	28 08.723	16 42.546
22	28 08.727	16 42.609
23	28 08.462	16 43.170
24	28 08.437	16 43.175
25	28 07.525	16 43.363
26	28 07.499	16 43.323

11.
QUEEN OF THE SOUTH

Wp	N	W
1	28 08.014	16 41.289
2	28 08.032	16 41.340
3	28 08.076	16 41.354
4	28 08.134	16 41.470
5	28 08.278	16 41.526
6	28 08.424	16 41.540
7	28 08.512	16 41.572
8	28 08.685	16 41.689
9	28 08.856	16 41.636
10	28 08.670	16 41.790
11	28 08.696	16 41.805
12	28 08.707	16 41.889
13	28 08.775	16 41.956
14	28 08.744	16 41.994
15	28 08.841	16 42.072
16	28 08.696	16 42.100
17	28 08.644	16 42.220
18	28 08.665	16 42.314
19	28 08.679	16 42.384

12.
WALKERS WHO LUNCH

Wp	N	W
1	28 07.029	16 39.812
2	28 06.468	16 40.539
3	28 06.326	16 40.617
4	28 06.218	16 40.641
5	28 06.142	16 40.697
6	28 05.942	16 40.737
7	28 05.944	16 40.597
8	28 05.895	16 40.155
9	28 05.890	16 39.900
10	28 05.494	16 39.505
11	28 05.393	16 39.428
12	28 05.311	16 39.534
17	28 06.399	16 41.318
18	28 06.415	16 41.139
19	28 06.520	16 41.079
20	28 06.792	16 41.045
21	28 06.901	16 40.973
22	28 07.077	16 40.902
23	28 07.207	16 40.984
24	28 07.351	16 41.055
25	28 07.438	16 41.066
26	28 07.810	16 41.041
27	28 07.870	16 41.210
28	28 08.054	16 41.154
29	28 08.017	16 41.295

13.
FANTASIA

Wp	N	W
1	28 07.642	16 41.388
2	28 07.371	16 41.333
3	28 07.242	16 41.300
4	28 07.105	16 41.294
5	28 06.995	16 41.324
6	28 06.961	16 41.366
7	28 06.853	16 41.472
8	28 06.779	16 41.496
9	28 06.541	16 41.621
10	28 06.501	16 41.684
11	28 06.437	16 41.606
12	28 06.429	16 41.609
13	28 06.370	16 41.510
14	28 06.444	16 41.384
15	28 06.412	16 41.366
16	28 06.364	16 41.373

14.
TABLE MOUNTAIN

Wp	N	W
1	28 05.982	16 40.836
2	28 06.036	16 40.986
3	28 06.005	16 41.124
4	28 05.976	16 41.147
5	28 05.982	16 41.208
6	28 06.017	16 41.271
7	28 05.970	16 41.291
8	28 05.958	16 41.323
9	28 05.952	16 41.364
10	28 05.973	16 41.391
11	28 05.912	16 41.411
12	28 05.889	16 41.421
13	28 05.889	16 41.447
14	28 05.898	16 41.465
15	28 05.899	16 41.505
16	28 05.848	16 41.700
17	28 05.937	16 41.802
18	28 05.962	16 41.768
19	28 06.037	16 41.783
20	28 06.057	16 41.784
21	28 06.066	16 41.793
22	28 06.173	16 41.801

- Bus times may change, so we advise you to collect the latest timetable from a TITSA bus station or Tourist Office.
- We include details only of those bus routes useful for getting to and from the walks in this book.
- **Bold text** indicates places on or near our walking routes.
- A 'Bono' bus ticket for 12 or 30 euros gives you reduced fares on any route, and is worthwhile if you intend using the bus service several times.
- Details of bus services can be found on www.titsa.com
- Some routes run reduced services on fiestas and at weekends.

112
SANTA CRUZ - ARONA
Santa Cruz - southern motorway - junctions of Caletillas - Candelaria - Güimar - Arico - Chimiche - Granadilla - and San Miguel - **Las Galletas** - **Guaza** junction - Buzanada junction - **Valle San Lorenzo** - **Arona**

SANTA CRUZ	ARONA
11.10	05.25
19.10	13.00
(Saturdays, Sundays, fiestas)	
11.30	5.25
19.45	14.00

325
PUERTO DE LA CRUZ - LOS GIGANTES
Puerto de la Cruz - Icod de los Vinos - **Santiago del Teide** - Los Gigantes

PUERTO DE LA CRUZ	LOS GIGANTES
6.20	8.40
8.40	10.55
10.40	12.55
14.40	17.15
16.45	19.10
19.15	21.25

342
PLAYA DE LAS AMÉRICAS - EL PORTILLO
Playa de las Américas - **Los Cristianos** - **Arona** - **La Escalona** - Vilaflor - **Parador de Turismo** - **Las Cañadas del Teide** - **El Portillo**

PLAYA DE LAS AMÉRICAS	EL PORTILLO
09.15 (A)	15.15 (B)

(A) Leaves Torviscas 15 min before this time, and at 09.30 from Los Cristianos
(B) Leaves from the cable car at 15.40, and from the Parador at 16.00

343
PUERTO DE LA CRUZ - PLAYA DE LAS AMÉRICAS
Puerto de la Cruz - El Botánico - northern motorway - southern motorway - **Los Cristianos** - **Playa de las Américas**

PUERTO DE LA CRUZ	PLAYA DE LAS AMÉRICAS (A)
09.00	09.00
11.10	11.30
15.20	15.30
17.35	17.45

(A) Leaves Torviscas 15 min before these times

345
PUERTO DE LA CRUZ - AGUAMANSA
Puerto de la Cruz - El Botánico - La Orotava - Camino de Chasna - **Aguamansa**

PUERTO DE LA CRUZ		AGUAMANSA	
05.30	(B)	06.00	
06.30	(B)	07.00	
07.00	(B)	07.30	
07.00		08.15	
08.45	(A)	09.50	(C)
09.35	(A)	10.50	(C)
10.20	(A)	11.35	(C)
11.15	(A)	12.20	(C)
11.45	(A)	12.55	(C)
12.30	(A)	13.50	(C)
13.15	(A)	14.25	(C)
14.00	(A)	15.15	(C)
15.00	(A)	16.15	(C)
15.45	(A)	16.55	(C)
16.30	(A)	17.45	(C)
17.15	(A)	18.20	(C)
18.00		19.15	
18.45		20.00	
19.35		20.45	(B)
20.15		21.15	
21.00	(B)		
23.30	(B)		

(A) To La Caldera
(B) To and from La Orotava
(C) Goes 5 min earlier from La Caldera

348
PUERTO DE LA CRUZ - LAS CAÑADAS DEL TEIDE (Parador)
Puerto de la Cruz - El Botánico - **La Orotava** - **Aguamansa** - **El Portillo** - **Las Cañadas del Teide (Parador)**

PUERTO DE LA CRUZ	LAS CAÑADAS DEL TEIDE (PARADOR)
9.15	16.00

355
BUENAVISTA - SANTIAGO DEL TEIDE
Buenavista - El Palmar - Las Portelas - El Carrizal - **Masca** - **Santiago del Teide**

from BUENAVISTA	from SANTIAGO DEL TEIDE
06.15	-
9.30	10.35
14.15	-
15.45	16.55

from MASCA to:

BUENAVISTA	SANTIAGO DEL TEIDE
6.45	-
10.55	10.05
15.00	-
17.15	16.15

392
ICOD DE LOS VINOS - PUERTO DE ERJOS
Icod de los Vinos - El Tanque - Ruigómez - **Puerto de Erjos**

ICOD DE LOS VINOS	PUERTO DE ERJOS
6.20	6.50
11.00	11.45
14.15	15.00

416
GRANADILLA - GUÍA DE ISORA
Granadilla - San Miguel - **Valle San Lorenzo** - La Camella - Cabo Blanco - Buzanada junction - **Los Cristianos** - Avda. del Ferry - **Playa de las Américas** - Torviscas - Tijoco junction - Tejina de Guía - Guía de Isora

GRANADILLA		GUÍA DE ISORA	
05.30		05.30	
05.45	(A)	06.30	
06.00		07.00	
06.30		07.25	
07.00		08.00	
07.30		08.25	
08.00		09.00	
08.30		09.45	
09.05		10.15	
09.35		10.45	
10.10		11.05	
10.40		11.35	
11.10		12.05	
11.40		12.35	
12.10		13.05	
12.40		13.30	
13.00	(C)	14.00	(A)
13.30		14.30	
14.00		15.30	
14.30		15.35	(C)
15.00		16.00	
15.30		16.30	
16.30		17.15	
16.50	(A)	17.45	
17.05		18.05	
17.45		18.45	
18.15		19.15	
18.45		19.45	
19.10		20.45	
19.40		20.40	
20.15		21.00	(C)
20.40	(C)	22.00	
21.00		22.45	(A)
00.35	(D)		

(Sat, Sun, fiestas)

GRANADILLA		GUÍA DE ISORA	
05.30		05.30	
05.45	(A)	06.30	
06.30		07.15	
07.30		08.25	
08.30	(B)	09.45	
09.35		10.45	(B)
10.40		11.35	
11.40		12.35	
12.40		13.30	
13.30		14.30	
14.30	(B)	15.30	
15.30		16.30	(B)
16.30		17.45	
17.45		18.45	
18.45		19.45	
19.40		20.40	
20.40	(C)	22.10	(C)
21.20	(A)		
00.35	(D)		

(A) From and to Los Cristianos - Guía de Isora
(B) Sat, Sun & fiestas from and to La Caleta
(C) Only as far as Playa de las Américas
(D) Los Cristianos - Adeje

441
LOS CRISTIANOS - LA CALETA
Los Cristianos - Avda. del Ferry - **Playa de las Américas** - Torviscas - Fañabe - **La Caleta**

LOS CRISTIANOS		LA CALETA	
06.50		07.30	
08.10		08.50	
09.00	(A,B)	09.45	(A)
09.55		10.30	
11.15		12.00	
12.55		13.40	
14.55		15.40	
15.30	(A)	16.45	(A)
16.30		17.20	
18.00		18.45	
19.55		20.40	

(A) Via Adeje
(B) Leaves from Playa de las Américas

442
PLAYA DE LAS AMÉRICAS - VALLE SAN LORENZO
Playa de las Américas - Avda. del Ferry - **Los Cristianos** - Chayofa - La Camella - Cabo Blanco - Buzanada junction - **Valle San Lorenzo** (*not Sat, Sun or fiestas*)

PLAYA DE LAS AMÉRICAS		VALLE SAN LORENZO	
08.00	(A)	08.30	(B)
09.30	(B)	10.30	(B)
14.30	(B)	15.30	(B,C)
16.30	(B,C)	17.30	(B,C)

(A) Playa de las Américas bus station - Chayofa - La Camella - Valle San Lorenzo
(B) Via Buzanada
(C) Via Centro de Salud El Mojón

450
PLAYA DE LAS AMÉRICAS - SAN ISIDRO
Playa de las Américas (bus station) - Avda. del Ferry - **Los Cristianos** - southern motorway - San Miguel junction - Reina Sofia airport junction - Granadilla junction - San Isidro (*not Sat, Sun or fiestas*)

PLAYA DE LAS AMÉRICAS	SAN ISIDRO
07.45	06.45
08.45	07.45
09.45	08.45
to	09.45
19.45	10.45
every 2 hours	to
	20.45
	every 2 hours

22.50	to
23.15	19.05
23.50	every 30/40 mins
00.15	19.40
	to
	22.40

460
ICOD DE LOS VINOS - PLAYA DE LAS AMÉRICAS
Icod de los Vinos - El Tanque - **Erjos** - **Santiago del Teide** - **Tamaimo** - Chío - Guía de Isora - Tijoco - **Adeje** - **Playa de las Américas**

ICOD DE LOS VINOS	PLAYA DE LAS AMÉRICAS
5.45	5.25
7.30	7.20
10.00	9.45
12.00	12.00
14.15	13.55
16.00	16.00
18.00	18.00
20.00	20.10

462
GUÍA DE ISORA - LOS GIGANTES
Guía de Isora - Chío - **Arguayo** - **Valle Santiago** - **Tamaimo** - Los Gigantes

GUÍA DE ISORA	LOS GIGANTES	
05.45	06.35	
08.00	08.50	
14.20	15.20	(B)
16.30 (A)	17.10	

(A) From Arguayo
(B) To Aruayo

467
PLAYA DE LAS AMÉRICAS - LAS GALLETAS
Playa de las Américas - Avda. del Ferry - **Los Cristianos** - **Las Galletas**

PLAYA DE LAS AMÉRICAS	LAS GALLETAS
06.40	06.20
07.00	06.35
08.00	07.05
09.00	07.45
10.00	to
to	13.05
22.00	every 30/40 mins
every 30/40 mins	14.05

470
GRANADILLA - PLAYA DE LAS AMÉRICAS
Playa de las Américas - Avda. del Ferry - **Los Crisitanos** - **Las Galletas** - **Golf del Sur** - **Los Abrigos** - El Médano - San Isidro - Granadilla

GRANADILLA		PLAYA DE LAS AMÉRICAS	
06.00	(A)	06.45	(A)
07.00		07.30	
07.05		to	
08.30		13.30	(A)
09.30		every 60 mins	
10.35		14.30	
11.30		15.30	
12.30		16.30	
13.30		to	
14.30	(A)	19.30	
to		every 60 mins	
17.30		20.40	
every 60 mins			
18.40			
19.30	(A)		
20.30			

(A) Does not stop at Golf del Sur

473
LAS GALLETAS - LOS GIGANTES
Las Galletas - **Los Cristianos** - Avda. del Ferry - **Playa de las Américas** - Torviscas - **Adeje** - Armeñime - Playa San Juan - Playa la Arena - Puerto Santiago - Los Gigantes

LAS GALLETAS		LOS GIGANTES	
05.25	(B)	06.15	
05.45	(B)	06.45	
06.00	(A)	07.15	(D)
06.15		07.45	
06.40		08.15	
06.45		08.45	
07.15		09.05	(C)
07.45		09.15	
08.10		09.25	(C)
to		09.45	
19.45		10.05	(C)
every 20 mins		10.15	
20.00		10.35	
20.45		11.05	
		to	
		20.05	
		every 20 mins	
		20.25	(A)
		20.45	(A,C)
		21.00	(A)
		21.20	(A)
		21.40	(A,C)

21.50		15.30	16.00
22.00	(C)	16.30	17.00
22.30		18.40	19.05
23.30		19.30	20.00
		20.30	21.00

(A) To and from Los Cristianos
(B) To and from Playa de las Américas
(C) Service only runs on working days
(D) Sat and Sun only, as far as Los Cristianos

(A) Continues to Playa de las Américas

480

ARONA - LOS CRISTIANOS
Arona - La Sabinita - La Camella - Chayofa - **Los Cristianos**

ARONA		LOS CRISTIANOS
05.45		06.00
06.55	(A)	08.00
08.30		09.00
09.30		10.00
10.30		11.00
12.30		13.05
13.30		14.00
14.30		15.00

482

VILAFLOR - LOS CRISTIANOS
Vilaflor - **La Escalona** - **Arona** - La Sabinita - La Camella - Chayofa - **Los Cristianos**

VILAFLOR		LOS CRISTIANOS
06.35	(A)	06.00
12.00		11.00
18.15		17.00

(A) Continues to Playa de las Américas

LA GUAGUA DE ADEJE

Town service runs from 7.30 to 21.00, Mondays to Fridays only. Operates in a figure of eight west-east around the town, every 20-25 minutes.

This glossary contains Spanish and Canarian words used in the text (shown in *italics* in this book), plus other local words that you may encounter.

A

abandonado	abandoned, in poor repair
abierto	open
acampamiento	camping
acantilado	cliff
acequia	water channel
agua	water
agua no potable	water (not drinkable)
agua potable	drinking water
alto	high
aparcamiento	parking
arroyo	stream
autopista	main road, motorway
ayuntamiento	town hall

B

bajo	low
barranco	ravine
bocadillo	bread roll
bodegón	inn
bosque	wood

C

cabezo	peak, summit
cabra	goat
cabrera	goatherd
caldera	collapsed volcanic cone
calima	hot sand/dust laden wind
calle	street
camino	trail, path, track
camino particular	private road
camino real	old donkey trail (lit. royal road)
camino rural	single track tarmacked road
cañadas	ravine
carretera	main road
casa	house
casa rural	country house

accommodation

cascada	waterfall
caserío	hamlet, village
cementario	cemetery
cerrado	closed
cerveza	beer
dos cerveza	one beer, and another one
choza	shelter
clinica	clinic, hospital
colmena	bee hive
comida	food
cordillera	mountain range
correos	post office
cortijo	farmstead
costa	coast
coto privado de caza	private hunting area
Cruz Roja	Red Cross (medical aid)
cuesta	slope
cueva	cave
cumbre	summit

D

degollado	pass
derecha	right (direction)
desprendimiento	landslide

E

embalse	reservoir
ermita	chapel
Espacio Naturaleza Protegido	protected area of natural beauty, 'pa'
estación de autobus	bus station

F

farmacia	chemist
faro	lighthouse
fiesta	holiday, celebration
finca	farm, country house
fuente	spring

G

gasolinera	petrol station
guagua	bus
Guardia Civil	police
guia	guide

H

hostal	hostel, accommodation
hoya	depression (geological)

I

iglesia	church
información	information
isla	island
izquierda	left (direction)

L

lago	lake
lavadero	laundry area (usually communal)
librería	bookshop
llano	plain
lluvioso	rainy
lomo	broad-backed ridge

M

malpais	'bad lands' wild, barren countryside
mapa	map
mercado	market
mirador	lookout/viewing point
montaña	mountain

N

nublado	cloudy

O

oficina de turismo	tourist office

P

pa	protected area of natural beauty
parapente	hang-glider
peligroso	danger
pensión	guesthouse
pico	peak
picon	black volcanic rock/sand
pista	dirt road/track
pista (forestal)	forest road/track
playa	beach
plaza	square
policia	police

pozo	well
prohibido el paso	no entry
puente	bridge
puerto	port, mountain pass

R

refugio	refuge, shelter
río	river, stream
roque	rock
ruta	route

S

salida	exit
senda	path, track
sendero	foot path
sierra	mountain range
sin salida	no through road/route
sirocco	hot dust/sand laden wind

T

tapas	bar snacks
tienda	shop
tipico	traditional bar/eating place
tormentoso	stormy
torre	tower
torrente	stream
tubería	water pipe

V

valle	valley
vega	meadow
ventoso	windy
volcán	volcano

Z

zona recreativa	recreation area

DISCOVERY WALKING GUIDES

34 WALKS

- a series of Walking Guide Books

We receive praise for our regional walking guide titles in almost every post. Thanks to the many happy users of these guides, DWG has acquired an enviable reputation for interesting and accurately described, walking routes. Now the time is right for our new **34 Walks** series of walking guide books. These new books are wider ranging than our previous guides, covering whole islands or regions. All the routes have been newly researched and even our 'classic' routes have been re-walked and rewritten to ensure that they are up-to-date.

Each title in the **34 Walks** series is designed to provide a wide range of interesting routes for moderately fit walkers, plus some routes for experienced walkers. Thanks to the feedback we receive from walkers we have designed these books so that you have the best walking guide book for the destination. Features in **34 Walks** books include:-

- walking route summary
- fully detailed walk descriptions including frequent timings
- GPS Waypoints (grid references) for all key points on a route
- detailed map at 1:25,000 or 1:40,000 scale for every walking route
- full GPS Waypoint lists for all the walking routes

Add in useful background information, and you have the best value walking guides that you can buy.

34 Walks books form one part of DWG's complete walking package. For each title there is also a **Tour & Trail Map**, or **Walkers' Maps** to complement each book.

Available from good book shops or by mail order. For up to date information on Discovery Walking Guides publications write to DWG Ltd, 10 Tennyson Close, Northampton NN5 7HJ, England or visit:-

www.walking.demon.co.uk or
www.dwgwalking.co.uk

Tour & Trail Maps were developed to meet the needs for accurate and up-to-date maps for destinations covered by Discovery Walking Guides. At the core of each **T&T** map design is a comprehensive ground-level survey carried out by car and on foot. The survey results are then translated into DWG's design programme, to produce a digital vector graphic database involving the organisation of several million pieces of information across a large number of 'layers' drawn digitally within our computers. Once a DWG digital vector graphic database has been established, new developments such as new roads and tracks, can be quickly incorporated into the correct layer of the database. Rapid updating, combined with state of the art 'file to plate' pre-press operation, enables DWG to produce new editions of **Tour & Trail Maps** quickly and efficiently.

Tour & Trail Maps have a Latitude/Longitude grid and datum information making them GPS compatible. DWG walking routes are clearly highlighted on **T&T** maps, along with their GPS Waypoints wherever space allows.

From 2003, all new **Tour & Trail Maps** titles will be produced on a super-durable material which is waterproof and tear-proof, making **T&T** maps the toughest maps available, in addition to being the most accurate and up-to-date.

Tour & Trail Maps are available for:-

- **Alpujarras**

- **Madeira**

- **La Gomera**

- **Gran Canaria Mountains**

- **Mallorca North & Mountains**

- **Menorca**

New to accompany our **34 Walks** series of guide books is a series of **Walkers' Maps** at a 1:25,000 scale, 4cms = 1km, a scale that is so popular for UK walking.

The interesting walking regions for destinations such as Lanzarote and Tenerife form pockets around the island, and a whole island **Tour & Trail Map** would not be viable; Tenerife at 1:40,000 scale would make a 3 metres by 2 metres map and Lanzarote would only be a bit smaller. Just try unfolding something that size while out on a walking route!

To solve the problem of providing top quality mapping at a pocketable size, we have developed **Walkers' Maps** which bring together the walking regions at 1:25,000 scale onto a single folded map at a size to fit your pocket. This gives you large scale maps for all the routes in a **34 Walks** guide book in one map product.

Tenerife Walkers' Maps will consist of 1:25,000 map sections covering routes in the South (4 map sections), West (one large map section), Las Cañadas/Teide (3 map sections) and the North (one large map section) plus an island locator map. The full **Tenerife Walkers' Map** and **Lanzarote Walkers' Map** are published in two editions; a low cost Paper edition and a Super-Durable waterproof and tearproof edition, using the same materials and techniques as for **Indestructible Maps**.

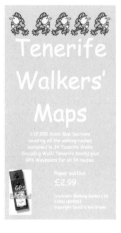

DRIVE! TOURING MAPS

Drive! Touring Maps are designed for today's drivers with the emphasis on accuracy and clarity. Using the digital vector graphic databases from our **Tour & Trail Maps**, plus specially commissioned surveys, **Drive! Touring Maps** are completely up to date on publication. Being up to date is important as Spain has recently changed its road numbering system, which makes driving very confusing if using an old map.

Special design criteria have been developed which result in exceptional clarity, while emphasising the motorist's needs for quick recognition of junctions, road numbers, petrol stations and refreshment stops with off-road parking.

Each **Drive! Touring Map** includes:-
- a comprehensive Place Name Index
- a Distance Chart for main destinations
- datum and grid information enabling the map to be used with modern GPS equipment

All this is backed up by:-
- large scale Street Plans which include Place Names Indexes for major resorts

Drive! Touring Maps include everything you need for exploring these exciting destinations by car.
Drive Touring Maps are available, or in development (D) for:-

- **Tenerife**

- **Lanzarote**

- **La Gomera** (D)

- **Gran Canaria** (D)

- **Fuerteventura** (D)

- **La Palma** (D)

- **Madeira**

- **Mallorca** (D)

- **Menorca**

PERSONAL NAVIGATOR FILES

Getting lost is not a pleasant experience, while getting lost in a foreign destination can be distinctly unpleasant. DWG have an excellent reputation for accurately researched and described walking routes, but even we can go further with our revolutionary **Personal Navigator Files**.

All DWG's **34 Walks** series of books are researched using modern GPS equipment, giving us an accuracy of better than five metres. GPS gives us extremely accurate walking routes, and DWG knows exactly where our authors have walked. Now we are making this GPS Track and Waypoint information available for GPS users in a range of formats to suit popular GPS software such as Oziexplorer, GPSY, Fugawi.

If you have a GPS, download lead and GPS software for your PC, then DWG's new **Personal Navigator Files** will mean that you can follow in the exact footsteps of our walking authors; now that really is 'vorsprung technik' for walkers.

Personal Navigator Files are available for:-

- **Alpujarras**

- **Tenerife**

- **Lanzarote**

- and will be available for all new **34 Walks** destinations. For more information, see DWG websites:-

www.walking.demon.co.uk
and
www.dwgwalking.co.uk

THE INDESTRUCTIBLE MAP COMPANY

INDESTRUCTIBLE MAPS

We've all suffered from maps that fall apart, split down the folds, and soak up water like a sponge. Sellotape, or better drafting tape, is pressed into service to repair the ailing paper map to try and make it last a bit longer. At DWG we believe in durability but even we admit that our paper maps have a limited life when subjected to the rigours of outdoors adventuring. So putting our money where our mouth is, we have formed **The Indestructible Map Company Ltd (TIMCo)**, which does exactly what it says in the name; it produces **Indestructible Maps** which are 'Guaranteed for Life'.

TIMCo combines DWG's expertise in researching and designing the best maps, with the latest materials technology and printing techniques, to produce the **Indestructible Map**. They tell us that the material is a 'high density polymer' core to which they fuse a printable layer of a China Clay type compound; well, they lost us somewhere around 'density' but we do know that what we have got is a map that in 'normal' use will last you a lifetime. It is waterproof, tear-proof, and just about proof to everything apart from fire and attack with sharp objects. You can fold it into a rain hat or beer glass - we've tried, so we know it works - and then still use it as the best map. It feels like silk but appears to have the strength of carbon fibre. You get all of these attributes in an **Indestructible Map** and all at a ridiculous price of £4.99.

Indestructible Maps are not easy to produce - otherwise all map publishers would be using these materials and techniques. Paper is easy. It has been around for hundreds of years and printing paper has been highly developed, plus paper is cheap. Specially coated high density polymer is expensive, eye-wateringly expensive. Printers don't like polymers; they have to run their machines more slowly (more expense), use special inks (very expensive) and put special dryers between each stage of the printing process.

On the first print run of **Tenerife Indestructible Map** our printers forgot some of the complex settings and 455 copies of **Tenerife Indestructible Map** fused themselves into a solid indestructible lump; unfortunately the printers dumped the mistake or we might have been short-listed for the Turner prize!

After all this, you have a lovely **Indestructible Map** as a flat sheet, but that is not the end of your problems. Folding an Indestructible material is a real problem as it always remembers that it once was a flat sheet; TIMCo have to keep the boxes of printed maps sealed until use otherwise we have a lot of flat maps which were once folded!

Enough of the moans and whinges about producing **Indestructible Maps** - just try one for yourself. We are convinced that TIMCo is the future of maps, and we will be using these materials and techniques for DWG's new **Tour & Trail Maps** and **Walkers' Maps**.

www.indestructiblemap.co.uk

WALKING IN THE CANARY ISLANDS

TENERIFE

Despite its 'tabloid' image Tenerife has some of the best walking routes and is suitable for a wide range of walking abilities, up to the most experienced mountain walkers. Once away from the tourist resorts and urban areas, walkers are rewarded with an extensive network of trails and *pistas* on which to explore the unspoilt landscapes. High altitude walking - 2,200 to 3,700 metres altitude - is available in the Las Cañadas/Mount Teide national park. The south and west of the island offer spectacular walking routes combined with easy access from the resorts, as does the upper Orotava Valley in the north. Further afield, the isolated Anaga peninsula will reward walkers prepared to make the long drive from the resorts.

Publications available :-
- **35 Tenerife Walks**
- **Walk! Tenerife South**
- **Tenerife Walkers' Maps - Paper Edition**
- **Tenerife Walkers' Maps - Super Durable Edition**
- **Tenerife Indestructible Map**
- **Drive! Tenerife Touring Map**

LA GOMERA

This national heritage island is a walking paradise with spectacular routes in all regions of La Gomera. Garajonay laurel forest is at the island's heart surrounded by huge *barrancos* offering walkers some of the best walking routes in the Canary Islands. Valle Gran Rey and Playa Santiago are developing as resorts but the rest of the island has been blissfully overlooked and offers the rural idyll many seek, if you are prepared for the laborious journey of a flight to Tenerife, transfer to Los Cristianos for ferry to La Gomera; best to book for two weeks or more to make the most of your time on our favourite island.

Publications available :-
- **34 La Gomera Walks**
- **La Gomera Tour & Trail Map**
- **Drive! La Gomera Touring Map**

LA PALMA

Spectacular La Palma is becoming better known, thanks to direct flights from Manchester and Gatwick, plus recent TV programmes. The world's steepest island rises direct from the sea to the high *cumbre* which forms the rim of the Taburiente. The island government has recently installed new waymarking posts and signs covering a wide range of routes. Very rewarding walking for the fitter walker.

LANZAROTE

The fire island is becoming more popular with leisure walkers. Despite having nothing over 700 metres in height, the desert and volcanic landscape contains a surprising variety of walking experiences. Escape from the intensively developed resorts and you will discover landscapes of a barren grandeur, plus a surprising variety of endemic plant life.

Publications available :-
- **19 Lanzarote Walks**
- **Lanzarote Walkers' Maps**
- **Lanzarote Indestructible Map**
- **Drive! Lanzarote Touring Map**

GRAN CANARIA

The best walking is some distance from the southern resorts, centred around Roque Nublo in the centre of the island and stretching westwards. Tremendous scenery amongst the massive canyons combines with a good network of trails to reward adventurous walkers.

Publications available :-
- **Gran Canaria Mountains Tour & Trail Map**
- **Gran Canaria Indestructible Map**
- **Drive Gran Canaria Touring Map**

EL HIERRO

The smallest and least known Canary Island has some of the most varied landscapes of any of the seven islands. Known to ancient mariners as the edge of the known world, it was once the home of the International Meridian which can still be seen on the western tip, before its move to Greenwich. Tiresome plane and ferry transfers mean that El Hierro has been overlooked by mass tourism, giving the island a Shangri-La quality for whose seeking peace and tranquillity. Interesting walking among varied landscapes far from the tourism crowds.

FUERTEVENTURA

'Strong Wind Island' is famous for its huge beaches, windsurfing and naturism. Most barren of the Canary Islands, there is little life outside of the resorts and island capital of Puerto Rosario. A few reasonable walking routes but generally this is an island more suited to Jeep Safari than walking.

Publications available :-
- **Fuerteventura Indestructible Map**
- **Drive! Fuerteventura Touring Map**

GPS THE EASY WAY

GPS
THE EASY WAY
BY
DAVID BRAWN

Ask not "What is GPS?"
Ask
"What can GPS do for me?"

GPS Advanced Use
'Spencer Raceway & Car Wreck Field'
Practical Exercise

Contents

Fr[...]
R[...]

B. Plotting Waypoints and Track

To give us a bit of a stroll before reaching the pub I plot the[...]
an almost circular route. With the map at 300% zoom I can [...]

navigation points of al[...]st and path
junctions down to a[...] accuracy of
which side of the [...] plan us to
walk along.

My planned route is, Wp1 ju[...]
Tennyson Close, and Broo[...]
Wp2 junction of Brook Lane [...]
Bartons Close, Wp3 Da[...]
village crossroads, Wp4 [...]
Dallington Park, Wp5 path [...]
in park. Wp6 corner of pa[...]
corner of park, Wp8 corner [...]
Wp9 start of alley to D[...]
Park Wp10 onto Dallingto[...]
W[...]ll Merthyr Road junct[...]
cross road here), Wp12 C[...]
Close junction, Wp13 Bro[...]
junction, Wp14 The Wheatsh[...]

Yes, I know that we could g[...]
pub by a quicker route but r[...]
the object of this exercise is[...]
Brian GPS Track Navigation[...]
as taking some refreshments[...]
ex[...]

Waypoint List

Map Name : No[...]hampton tf
Map File : [...]NorthamptonUTM

Datum : [...]rd Srvy Grt Brtn

Waypoint[...] : C:\GPS\DallingtonPark.wpt

21/01/03 17:51:44

Num	Name	Zone	Easting	Northing	Alt(ft)	Description
1	1	30U	642183	5790419		junc Tennyson Close
2	2	30U	642085	5790539		junc The Bartons
3	3	30U	642012	5790447		village X roads
4	4	30U	641939	5790339		edge of park
5	5	30U	641953	5790325		path junction
6	6	30U	641867	5790107		corner of park
7	7	30U	642068	5789670		corner of park
8	8	30U	642224	5790055		corner of park
9	9	30U	642245	5790073		start of narrow alley
10	10	30U	642281	5790101		Dallington Road
11	11	30U	642254	5790144		junc Merthyr Road
12	12	30U	642198	5790192		junc Cardigan Close
13	13	30U	642105	5790295		junc Brook Lane
14	14	30U	642070	5790349		The Wheatsheaf

£4.99

from good bookshops,
amazon.co.uk,
or post free direct from

DWG
10 Tennyson Close
Northampton NN5 7HJ

ISBN 1-899554-46-7

TRADE-UP TO DWG'S NEW TITLES

35 **Tenerife** Walks, 34 **Alujarras** Walks and 34 **Menorca** Walks guide books are a huge advance on our original 'map-fold with plastic wallet' walking guides.

DWG believes in recycling our old titles when they are replaced by the new guide books, so we would like to offer you a Trade-In value on our old titles when you Trade-Up to the new titles.

DWG's 'Trade-Up' to New Titles with 'Trade-In' Values for the titles being replaced will apply to our new titles as they are published. See websites for current information.

For each **Alpujarras**, **Menorca** or **Tenerife** map-fold guide you send in with your order, we will give you a £2.00 Trade-In value against the new title.

Keep the plastic wallet (useful for travel documents) and simply send in parts 1 & 2 of the guide and deduct £2.00.

Please note 'Trade-In' values only apply to titles ordered direct from DWG. These offers are not available in book shops or via internet book sellers.

Titles	Price	less £2.00 Trade-In
34 Alpujarras Walks	£9.99 post free	£7.99 post free
35 Tenerife Walks	£9.99 post free	£7.99 post free
Tenerife Walkers' Maps	£4.99 post free	£2.99 post free
34 Menorca Walks	£6.99 post free	£4.99 post free

Send you order, complete with your name and address, parts 1 & 2 of the guide and your cheque to:-

Discovery Walking Guides Ltd
10 Tennyson Close
Northampton NN5 7HJ

- and we will post your new title(s) straight back to you.

INDEX OF PLACE NAMES

PLANTS AND FLOWERS

For the enthusiast, a 'bible' of flowering plants of the Canary Islands 'Flores Silvestres de Las Islas Canarias', (authors David and Zoé Bramwell, published by Editorial Rueda of Madrid, ISBN 84-7207-062-X) provides the most comprehensive information, although this is not always available in English translation.

WILDLIFE

A weighty tome, in Spanish but liberally illustrated, is 'Naturaleza de las Islas Canarias' (published by Turquesa, ISBN 84-95412-18-17) should satisfy the keenest wildlife specialist.

For these titles and other Canary Islands books and maps try Libreria Barbara, Calle General Franco, 38650 Los Cristianos, Tel/Fax: 922 792301 (PO Box 216, 38650 Los Cristianos)

USEFUL PHONE NUMBERS & ADDRESSES

N.B.
All Tenerife numbers are prefixed by **922**, with the exception of the emergency numbers.

When dialling from outside Spain, prefix the number with **00 34**

Emergencies	
(pan-European number)	
Fire, police, ambulance, civil defence	**112**
Policia Nacional	**091**
Policia Local	**092**
Guardia Civil	**062**
Urgencias Salud	**061**
(medical emergencies)	

Taxis	
Adeje area	**922 741612**
Arona area	**922 790352**
Los Cristianos	**922 796611**
Playa de las Américas	**922 714468**

There are plenty of taxis in the larger towns. Most villages have a public telephone, and some bars have a pay phone. Bar owners will usually phone for a taxi on your behalf, but buy a drink too.

Tourist Information Offices

UK
Oficina Española de Turismo
22-23 Manchester Square
London W1M 5AP
020 7486 8077

www.tourspain.es
londres@tourspain.es

TENERIFE
Oficina De Turismo Cabildo
Insular
Plaza España
E-38003 **922 60 58 00**
S. C. de Tenerife **922 23 95 92**

Oficina De Turismo
General Franco
Los Cristianos **922 75 71 37**

Oficina De Turismo
Av. Rafael Puig Lluvina 1
Costa Adeje **922 75 06 33**

There are also Tourism Offices at the beaches of Playa Fañabe, Playas Troya, and Playa las Vistas. For exact locations, see the Playa de las Américas/Los Cristianos street plan on either the **Drive! Tenerife Touring Map** or **Tenerife Indestructible Map**.